Elhanan Winchester

A Choice Collection of Hymns

From Various Authors Adapted to Public Worship

Elhanan Winchester

A Choice Collection of Hymns
From Various Authors Adapted to Public Worship

ISBN/EAN: 9783337289935

Printed in Europe, USA, Canada, Australia, Japan

Cover: Foto ©Thomas Meinert / pixelio.de

More available books at **www.hansebooks.com**

A

COLLECTION

OF

HYMNS,

FROM

VARIOUS AUTHORS,

ADAPTED TO

PUBLICK WORSHIP:

DESIGNED FOR THE EDIFICATION OF THE PIOUS OF ALL DENOMINATIONS; BUT MORE PARTICULARLY FOR THE USE OF THE BAPTIST CHURCH IN PHILADELPHIA.

PHILADELPHIA:
PRINTED BY ENOCH STORY, Jun. LIVING IN STRAWBERRY-ALLEY. 1784.

A COLLECTION OF HYMNS.

HYMN I. *Gratitude to God.*

1. WHEN all thy mercies, O my God,
  My rising foul surveys;
Transported with the view I'm loſt
  In wonder, love, and praiſe.

2. O how ſhall words with equal warmth
  The gratitude declare,
Which glows within my raviſh'd heart?
  But thou canſt read it there.

3. Thy providence my life ſuſtain'd,
  And all my wants redreſs'd,
When in the ſilent womb I lay,
  And hung upon the breaſt.

4. To all my weak complaints and cries,
   Thy mercy lent an ear,
Ere yet my feeble thoughts had learn'd
   To form themselves in pray'r.

5. Unnumber'd comforts on my soul
   Thy tender care bestow'd,
Before my infant heart conceiv'd
   From whence those comforts flow'd.

6. When in the slipp'ry paths of youth
   With heedless steps I ran,
Thine arm unseen convey'd me safe,
   And led me up to man.

7. Thro' hidden dangers, toils, and deaths,
   It gently clear'd my way;
And thro' the pleasing snares of vice,
   More to be fear'd than they.

8. When worn with sickness, oft hast thou
   With health renew'd my face;
And, when in sins and sorrows sunk
   Reviv'd my soul with grace.

9. (Thy bounteous hand with worldly bliss
   Hath made my cup run o'er,
And in a kind and faithful friend
   Has doubled all my store.)

10. Ten thousand thousand precious gifts
    My daily thanks employ;
Nor is the least a chearful heart,
    That tastes those gifts with joy.

11. Thro'

11. Thro' ev'ry period of my life,
   Thy goodness I'll pursue;
And after death in distant worlds,
   The glorious theme renew.

12. When nature fails, and day and night
   Divide thy works no more,
My ever grateful heart, O Lord,
   Thy mercy shall adore.

13. Thro' all Eternity to thee
   A joyful song I'll raise;
For oh! Eternity alone
   Can utter all thy praise.

H Y M N II.

1. DEAR Lord, how wond'rous is thy love
   To such unworthy worms as we!
Thou hast sent down the heav'nly Dove,
   To set our souls at liberty.

2. We that were doom'd to woe and pain,
   Expos'd to death of ev'ry kind,
Thro' Jesus Christ, the Lamb once slain,
   Do life, and peace, and pardon find.

3. Shall we forget our Saviour's grace,
   Who dy'd to save our guilty souls,
And bring us to his Father's face,
   Where endless peace and pleasure rolls?

4. Forbid, O Lord, each wand'ring thought,
   May Christ be all in our esteem;

Let earthly things be all forgot,
  And counted lofs, compar'd with him.

5. Lord Jefus, make us bear in mind
  Thy rich thy pure redeeming love,
'Till we fhall be for ever join'd
  With thofe that fing thy praife above:

6. Then fhall we ftand before thy face,
  And fhout with all the ranfom'd throng;
Our cry fhall be, " Free Grace, Free Grace,"
  While endlefs ages roll along.

HYMN III. *For the laft day of the year.*

1. O Praife the Lord of Heav'n,
    Whofe mercy never fails;
  Six troubles come, and alfo fev'n,
   But ftill his grace prevails.

2. The year that's almoft paft
    His goodnefs did proclaim;
  His love doth now and always laft,
    Give glory to his name.

3. How wond'rous are his ways
    Which he to us makes known!
  We join to fing our Maker's praife,
    And worfhip him alone.

4. When we the year begun
    We rais'd our chearful fongs;
  And furely when its courfe is run
    To God our praife belongs.

5. His

5. His mercies still are new,
   Let us extol his love;
May we this blessed theme pursue
   Till we shall meet above.

HYMN IV. *On the death of a Saint.*

1. BLESSED are they (the scriptures say)
      That dying win the prize,
For rest they shall, their good works all
   Do follow them likewise.

2. Death's but a sleep, why should we weep
      For those in Christ who die?
Since this we know, to peace they go,
   And joys possess on high.

3. Altho' to dust their bodies must
      Be turn'd beneath the clod,
Yet they shall rise above the skies,
   And ever live with God.

4. Christ will aloud before the croud
      Compos'd of Adam's race,
Confess them dear, who own'd him here,
   And bore for him disgrace.

5. Robes they shall have that will outbrave
      The whiteness of the snow;
Most pure and bright, like shining light;
   Such Jesus will bestow.

6. Then why need we dejected be?
      Our loss is their great gain;

For

For they shall stand at Christ's right hand,
  And with their Saviour reign.

7. Their happy days are spent in praise,
  While here we sigh and groan;
Could we but see how blest they be,
  'Twould make us cease to moan.

8. If there was end, 'twould trouble send,
  And would eclipse the joy,
But 'tis not so, they'll never go
  Out of that sweet employ:

9. When they've been there ten million years,
  And millions more are done,
They've no less days to sing God's praise
  Than when they first begun.

HYMN V. *The Lord will provide*

1. THO' troubles assail,
  And dangers affright,
Tho' friends should all fail,
  And foes all unite;
Yet one thing secures us,
  Whatever betide,
The Scripture assures us,
  " The Lord will provide."

2. The birds without barn
  Or storehouse are fed,
From them let us learn
  To trust for our bread:

His saints, what is fitting,
   Shall ne'er be deny'd,
So long as 'tis written
   " The Lord will provide."

3. We may, like the ships,
   By tempests be tost
On perilous deeps,
   But cannot be lost:
Tho' Satan enrages
   The wind and the tide,
The promise engages,
   " The Lord will provide."

4. His call we obey
   Like Abra'm of old,
Not knowing our way,
   But faith makes us bold;
For tho' we are strangers
   We have a good guide,
And trust in all dangers,
   " The Lord will provide."

5. When Satan appears
   To stop up our path,
And fill us with fears,
   We triumph by faith;
He cannot take from us,
   Tho' oft' he has try'd,
This heart cheering promise,
   " The Lord will provide."

6. He tells us we're weak,
   Our hope is in vain,

The good that we seek
  We ne'er shall obtain;
But when such suggestions
  Our spirits have ply'd,
This answers all questions,
  " The Lord will provide."

7. No strength of our own,
  Or goodness we claim,
Yet since we have known
  The Saviour's great name,
In this our strong tower
  For safety we hide,
The Lord is our power,
  " The Lord will provide."

8. When life sinks apace,
  And death is in view,
This word of his grace
  Shall comfort us thro':
No fearing or doubting
  With Christ on our side,
We hope to die shouting,
  " The Lord will provide."

HYMN VI. *Esau.*

1. POOR Esau repented too late,
  That once he his birth-right despis'd;
And sold, for a morsel of meat,
  What could not too highly be priz'd:
How great was his anguish when told
  The *blessing* he sought to obtain,
Was gone with the *birth-right* he sold,
  And none could recall it again!   2. He

2. He stands as a warning to all,
   Wherever the gospel shall come;
O hasten and yield to the call,
   While yet for repentance there's room!
Your season will quickly be past,
   Then hear, and obey it to-day;
Lest when you seek mercy at last,
   The Saviour should frown you away.

3. What is it the world can propose?
   A morsel of meat at the best!
For this are you willing to lose
   A share in the joys of the blest?
Its pleasures will speedily end,
   Its favour and praise are but breath:
And what can its profits befriend
   Your soul in the moment of death?

4. If Jesus for these you despise,
   And sin to the Saviour prefer,
In vain your entreaties and cries,
   When summon'd to stand at his bar:
How will you his presence abide?
   What anguish will torture your heart?
The saints all enthron'd by his side,
   And you be compell'd to depart!

5. Too often, dear Saviour, have I
   Preferr'd some poor trifle to thee;
How is it thou dost not deny
   The blessing and birth right to me?
No better than Esau I am,
   Tho' pardon and heaven be mine;
To me belongs nothing but shame,
   The praise and the glory be thine.

HYMN

HYMN VII.

What think ye of Christ?

1. WHAT think you of Christ? is the test
  To try both your state and your scheme;
You cannot be right in the rest,
  Unless you think rightly of him.
As Jesus appears in your view,
  As he is beloved or not;
So God is disposed to you
  And mercy or wrath are your lot.

2. Some take him a creature to be,
  A man, or an angel at most;
Sure these have not feelings like me,
  Nor know themselves wretched and lost:
So guilty, so helpless, am I,
  I durst not confide in his blood,
Nor on his protection rely,
  Unless I were sure he is God.

3. Some stile him The Pearl of great Price,
  And say, " He's the Fountain of Joys;"
Yet feed upon folly and vice,
  And cleave to the world, and its toys:
Like Judas the Saviour they kiss,
  And while they salute him betray;
Ah! what will profession like this
  Avail in his terrible day?

4. If ask'd, what of Jesus I think?
  Tho' still my best thoughts are but poor;

I say, He's my meat and my drink,
  My life, and my strength, and my store:
My Shepherd, my Husband, my Friend,
  My Saviour from sin and from thrall;
My hope from beginning to end,
  My Portion, my Lord, and my All.

H Y M N   VIII.

1. BY whom was David taught
    To aim the dreadful blow,
When he Goliath fought,
    And laid the Gittite low?
Nor sword nor spear the stripling took,
But chose a pebble from the brook.

2. 'Twas Israel's God and King,
    Who sent him to the fight;
Who gave him strength to fling,
    And skill to aim aright.
Ye feeble saints, your strength endures,
Because young David's God is yours.

3. Who order'd Gideon forth,
    To storm th' invaders camp,
With arms of little worth,
    A pitcher and a lamp?
The trumpets made his coming known,
And all the host was overthrown.

4. Oh! I have seen the day
    When with a single word,
God helping me to say
    " My trust is in the Lord;"

B

My soul has quell'd a thousand foes,
Fearless of all that would oppose.

5. But unbelief, self-will,
　　Self-righteousness and pride;
　How often do they steal
　　My weapon from my side?
Yet David's Lord, and Gideon's Friend,
Will help his servant to the end.

HYMN IX.

Faith, is a comprehensive sense.

1. SIGHT, hearing, feeling, taste and smell,
　　Are gifts we highly prize;
But faith does singly each excel,
　　And all the five comprize,

2. More piercing than the eagle's sight
　　It views the world unknown;
Surveys the glorious realms of light
　　And Jesus on the throne.

3. It hears the mighty voice of God,
　　And ponders what he saith;
His word and works, his gifts and rod,
　　Have each a voice to faith.

4. It feels the touch of heav'n's pow'r,
　　And from that boundless source,
Derives fresh vigor ev'ry hour,
　　To run its daily course,

5. The truth and goodnefs of the Lord,
  Are fuited to its tafte;
Mean is the worldlings pamper'd board,
  To faith's perpetual feaft.

6. It fmells the dear Redeemer's name
  Like ointment poured forth;
Faith only knows or can proclaim,
  Its favor or its worth.

7. Till faving faith poffefs the mind,
  In vain of fenfe we boaft;
We are but fenfelefs, taftelefs, blind,
  And deaf, and dead, and loft.

HYMN X.

Jofeph made known to his brethren.

1. WHEN Jofeph his brethren beheld,
    Afflicted, and trembling with fear,
His heart with compaffion was fill'd,
  From weeping he could not forbear:
A while his behaviour was rough,
  To bring their paft fin to their mind;
But when they were humbled enough,
  He hafted to fhew himfelf kind.

2. How little they thought it was he,
  Whom they had ill treated and fold!
How great their confufion muft be,
  As foon as his name he had told!
" I'm Jofeph your brother (he faid)
" And ftill to my heart you are dear,
              " You

" You fold me, and thought I was dead,
  " But God, for your fakes, fent me here."

3. Tho' greatly diftreffed before,
   When charg'd with purloining the cup,
They now were confounded much more,
   Not one of them durft to look up.
" Can Jofeph, whom we would have flain,
  " Forgive us the evil we did?
  " And will he our houfholds maintain?
  " O this is a brother indeed!"

4. Thus dragg'd by my confcience, I came
   And laden with guilt, to the Lord;
Surrounded with terror and fhame,
   Unable to utter a word.
At firft he look'd ftern and fevere,
   What anguifh then pierced my heart!
Expecting each moment to hear
   The fentence, " Thou curfed depart!"

5. But oh! What furprize when he fpoke,
   While tendernefs beam'd in his face,
My heart then to pieces was broke,
   O'erwhelm'd and confounded with grace:
" Poor finner, I know thee full well,
  " By thee I was fold and was flain;
  " I dy'd to redeem thee from hell,
   And raife thee in glory to reign.

6. I'm Jefus whom thou haft blafphem'd,
  " And crucify'd often afrefh;
  " But let me henceforth be efteem'd

" Thy

" Thy brother, thy bone, and thy flesh:
" My pardon I freely bestow,
  " Thy wants I will fully supply;
" I'll guide thee and guard thee below,
  " And soon will remove thee on high.

7. Go publish to sinners around,
  " (That they may be willing to come)
" The mercy which now you have found,
  " And tell them that yet there is room."
Oh, sinners the message obey!
No more vain excuses pretend;
But come, without farther delay,
  To Jesus our brother and friend.

HYMN XI.

The Christian's farewel; or dying saint's song.

1. FAREWEL, dear friends in Christ below,
    I bid you all a short adieu:
My time is come, I long to go;
    I trust I soon my Lord shall view.

2. I thank you for your kindness shown,
    My Jesus will reward you all;
I leave you with the Lord alone.
    'Till he from earth your souls shall call.

3. Farewel dear neighbours, brethren, friends,
    I hope we soon shall meet with joy;

B 3

My

My heav'nly Father for me sends,
   I go where nothing can annoy.

4. Adieu, to you mine enemies,
   You that have fought to do me harm
By slander, envy, rage and lies,
   But God upheld me with his arm:

5. I wish you all eternal life,
   I owe you not the least ill-will;
My soul is free from wrath and strife,
   Tho' me you hate, I love you still.

6. Adieu, thou sun, ye stars, and moon,
   No longer shall I need your light;
My God's my Sun, he makes my noon,
   My day shall never change to night.

7. Adieu, to all things here below,
   Vain world, I leave thy fleeting toys;
Adieu to sin, fear, pain and woe,
   And welcome bright eternal joys.

8. Temptations, troubles, griefs, adieu;
   Sorrows becloud my face no more:
I go to pleasures ever new,
   Where toils, and strifes, and wars are o'er.

9. Now I have done with earthly things;
   And all to come is boundless bliss;
My eager spirit spreads her wings;
   Jesus says "Come;" I answer "Yes."

10. Weep

10. Weep not dear friends: I tell you all
   I go to dwell with Christ on high;
I hear my blessed Saviour's call,
   And trusting in his promise die.

11. Father, I come to thee above,
   All things below I leave behind;
The fountain of eternal love
   Is open'd to my joyful mind.

12. Eternity! transporting found!
   While God exists my heav'n remains!
Fullness of joy that knows no bound
   Shall make my soul forget her pains.

HYMN XII.

1. THE praise of God shall fill my soul
      While I have breath, or use my voice;
And while eternal ages roll
   In Christ my Lord I will rejoice.

2. O may I never stop to rest
   Till I shall come to God on high,
Till I shall lean on Jesu's breast,
   And my dear Saviour magnify.

3. Then shall the wonders of his name
   Constrain my joyful soul to sing;
I shall eternally proclaim
   The glories of the Almighty King.

4. The

4. The voice of endless harmony
   My ravish'd soul with joy shall hear;
No discord in the melody,
   No jarring sounds shall strike mine ear.

HYMN XIII.

1. CAN such poor feeble worms as we
     Praise and adore our Saviour's name?
Or bring a tribute Lord to thee?
   Or half thy pow'r and love proclaim?

2. We stand amaz'd, when we behold
   Thy glory and thy beauty Lord!
Thy love and grace can ne'er be told,
   Which thou to mortals dost afford.

3. Yet Lord, we would attempt thy praise,
   We would exalt thy holy name;
Lord, we would walk in thy sweet ways;
   And sing, and tell thy wond'rous fame.

4. Fain would our souls mount up to thee,
   And feast forever on thy love;
And praise the sacred Deity,
   As Angels do that dwell above.

HYMN XIV.

1. SAVIOUR of men, we bless thy name,
     For thou art good forevermore;
Thy pow'r and grace we would proclaim,
   And thine eternal love adore.

2. Thy

2. Thy glory shall forever stand,
    Thy truth remains both firm and sure;
Our souls we venture in thine hand,
    And there we know we are secure.

3. Tho' troubles come and sorrows rise,
    We will not fear for God's our aid;
Ill tidings cannot these surprize
    Who are upon Jehovah stay'd.

4. Glory to Christ our faithful friend;
    (He is the Lord whom Angels fear)
On him we always would depend,
    And in his righteousness appear.

5. We love the Lord our God most high,
    His grace demands our noblest song;
All praise to Christ who came to die,
    To him all glory doth belong.

HYMN XV.

1. THE saints appear to tread the courts
    Of their dear God below;
Behold the multitude resorts
    To hear the trumpet blow.

2. Lord God, appear for our relief,
    What can we do alone?
Come Saviour, banish unbelief,
    And take us for thine own.

3. Our eyes O Lord, are unto thee,
　Aſſiſt us, Lord, we pray;
O may thy ſpirit preſent be!
　O Lord, thy power diſplay.

4. Jeſus, let us thy goſpel hear,
　Teach us to know thy voice;
Make ev'ry ſtubborn ſinner fear,
　And all thy ſaints rejoice.

5. Come Lord, nor let us be diſmay'd;
　Lord, hear thy people pray;
And let thy mercy be diſplay'd
　Amongſt us here this day.

6. May ſinners hear thy pow'rful call,
　And thy Salvation ſee;
So ſhall our hearts, both one and all,
　Sing ſongs of praiſe to thee.

HYMN XVI.

1. 'TIS pleaſure, Lord, on thee to wait;
　We come to ſeek our God again;
We now ſtand watching at thy gate;
　To ſerve the Lord is ne'er in vain.

2. Afford us Lord thy ſpecial grace,
　That we may praiſe thy name aright,
And run with joy the heav'nly race,
　Thro' faith and patience with delight.

3. O may we truſt in thee alone,
　For thou haſt help'd us hitherto;

　　　　　　　　　　　　　　And

And since thy name to us is known,
May we thy ways with zeal pursue.

HYMN XVII.

Hannah: Or the Throne of Grace.

1. WHEN *Hannah* press'd with grief,
    Pour'd forth her soul in pray'r;
She quickly found relief,
    And left her burthen there:
Like her in ev'ry trying case,
Let us approach the throne of grace.

2. When she began to pray
    Her heart was pain'd and sad;
But ere she went away,
    Was comforted and glad:
In trouble, what a resting place,
Have they who know the throne of grace.

3. Tho' men and Devils rage,
    And threaten to devour;
The saints from age to age,
    Are safe from all their pow'r:
Fresh strength they gain to run their race,
By waiting at the throne of grace.

4. *Eli* her case mistook,
    How was her spirit mov'd
By his unkind rebuke?
    But God her cause approv'd.

We need not fear a creature's face,
While welcome at the throne of grace.

5. She was not fill'd with wine,
    (As *Eli* rashly thought)
But with a faith divine,
    And found the help she sought:
Tho men despise and call us base,
Still let us ply the throne of grace.

6. Men have not pow'r or skill,
    With troubled souls to bear;
Tho' they express good-will,
    Poor comforters they are:
But swelling sorrows sink apace,
When we approach the throne of grace.

7. Numbers before have try'd,
    And found the promise true;
Nor one been yet deny'd,
    Then why should I or you?
Let us by faith their footsteps trace,
And hasten to the throne of grace.

8. As fogs obscure the light,
    And taint the morning air,
But soon are put to flight,
    If the bright sun appear;
Thus Jesus will our sorrows chase,
By shining from the throne of grace.

HYMN

HYMN XVIII.

Travelling in birth for souls.

1. WHAT contradictions meet
    In ministers employ!
It is a bitter sweet,
    A sorrow full of joy:
No other post affords a place
For equal honor, or disgrace!

2. Who can describe the pain
    Which faithful preachers feel;
Constrain'd to speak, in vain,
    To hearts as hard as steel?
Or who can tell the pleasures felt,
When stubborn hearts begin to melt?

3. The Saviour's dying love,
    The soul's amazing worth,
Their utmost efforts move,
    And draw their bowels forth:
They pray and strive, their rest departs,
Till Christ be form'd in sinners hearts.

4. If some small hope appear,
    They still are not content;
But, with a jealous fear,
    They watch for the event:
Too oft they find their hopes deceiv'd,
Then, how their inmost souls are griev'd!

5. But when their pains succeed,
      And from the tender blade
The rip'ning ears proceed,
      Their toils are overpaid:
No harvest joy can equal theirs,
To find the fruit of all their cares.

6. On what has now been sown
      Thy blessing, Lord, bestow;
The pow'r is thine alone,
      To make it spring and grow:
Do thou the gracious harvest raise,
And thou, alone, shalt have the praise.

HYMN XIX.

Praise to the Creator.

1. ETERNAL Majesty on high,
      Thou God of pow'r and love,
Thy hands have spread the starry sky,
      And form'd the worlds above.

2. This globe below shews forth thy might,
      Thy goodness and thy skill;
The sun, the moon, the day, and night,
      Thy pleasure do fulfil.

3. Beasts, birds, fish, insects all declare
      Thou art the mighty God;
Fire, hail, and storms, earth, water, air,
      Declare thy name abroad.

4. Trees, mountains, rivers, rocks, and plains,
      Gardens, and fruitful lands,

Proclaim " The God of goodnefs reigns;"
  And will while nature ſtands.

5, All things below, and all above,
  God, wife, good, great proclaim;
Then let the children of his love
  Delight to blefs his name.

6. The heav'nly Father, and the Son,
  And Spirit we adore;
'Tis now as 'twas when time begun,
  And ſhall be evermore.

HYMN XX.

1. O Lord, thou know'ſt my foul's defires,
    And thou canſt give me perfect eafe;
Thou art the good my heart admires,
    There's nothing but thy love can pleafe.

2. Give me, O Lord, the happinefs
    To fit and hear thy gracious voice;
Come, Saviour, come, my foul poffefs,
    And make my mourning heart rejoice.

3. Lord, I would praife thy holy name,
    Thou art my everlaſting friend;
Thou haſt not put my foul to ſhame;
    Preferve me fafe unto the end.

4. Thou art my ſtrength, and my fupport,
    My hope, my everlaſting aid;
To thee I always would refort,
    And truſt in thee when I'm afraid.

5. Thy

5. Thy name affords my foul relief,
   When I with forrows am oppreſt;
When I am full of woe and grief,
   Thy word doth give my ſpirit reſt.

6. Teach me to do thy holy will,
   Unite my heart to fear thy name;
O lead me to thy heav'nly hill,
   Where ſtands the new Jeruſalem.

7. Were not the Lord of hoſts my ſtrength
   I ſhould have funk in deep deſpair;
But now I truſt I ſhall at length
   Arrive at Canaan's harbour fair:

8. There ſhall I reſt for evermore,
   Fearleſs of ſtorms, and raging ſeas,
And fit upon the heav'nly ſhore,
   And dwell at everlaſting eaſe.

HYMN XXI.

1. ETERNAL God, thy pow'r make known,
      Make the whole earth confeſs
That thou art God, and thou alone
   Doſt rule in righteouſneſs.

2. May the whole earth thy glory ſee,
   And thy falvation know;
And to thy faints, who wait for thee,
   Thy works and wonders ſhow.

3. Lord Jeſus, come, and take thy pow'r,
   And rule us by thy grace;

We wait for that expected hour
   When we shall see thy face.

4. Our souls are longing for the day
   When Jesus shall be king;
When he our stubborn sins shall slay,
   And we his praise shall sing.

5. Our hearts rejoice in Jesu's name,
   His word forbids our fear;
We love his gospel to proclaim
   That all mankind may hear:

6. But dearest Lord, let us enjoy
   That everlasting peace,
That nothing ever shall destroy,
   Nor cause it to decrease.

7. Lord here we wait to know thy will,
   And to obey the same;
May we our course on earth fulfil,
   In honor to thy name.

HYMN XXII.

Jericho; or the waters healed.

1. THO' Jericho pleasantly stood,
   And look'd like a promising soil;
The harvest produc'd little food,
   To answer the husbandman's toil:
The water some property had,
   Which poisonous prov'd to the ground;

The springs were corrupted and bad,
  The streams spread a barrenness round.

2. But soon by the cruise and the salt,
  Prepar'd by Elisha's command,
The water was cur'd of its fault,
  And plenty enriched the land:.
An emblem sure this of the grace
  On fruitless dead sinners bestow'd;
For man is in Jericho's case,
  Till cur'd by the mercy of God.

3. How noble a creature he seems!
  What knowledge, invention, and skill!
How large and extensive his schemes!
  How much can he do if he will!
His zeal to be learned and wise,
  Will yield to no limits or bars;
He measures the earth and the skies,
  And numbers and marshals the stars.

4. Yet still he is barren of good;
  In vain are his talents and art;
For sin has infected his blood,
  And poison'd the streams of his heart:
The Cockatrice eggs he can hatch,
  Or, spider-like, cobwebs can weave;
'Tis madness to labour and watch
  For what will destroy or deceive.

5. But grace, like the salt in the cruise,
  When cast in the spring of the soul,
A wonderful change will produce,
  Diffusing new life thro' the whole:

The

The wildernefs blooms like a rofe,
    The heart which was vile and abhorr'd,
Now fruitful and beautiful grows,
    The garden and joy of the Lord.

HYMN XXIII.

1. JOY is a fruit that will not grow
    In nature's barren foil;
All we can boaft, 'till Chrift we know,
    Is vanity and toil.

2. But where the Lord has planted grace,
    And made his glories known;
There fruits of heav'nly joy and peace
    Are found, and there alone.

3. A bleeding Saviour feen by faith,
    A fenfe of pard'ning love,
A hope that triumphs over death,
    Give joys like thofe above.

4. To take a glimpfe within the vail,
    To know that God is mine;
Are fprings of joy that never fail,
    Unfpeakably divine.

5. Thefe are the joys that fatisfy,
    And fanctify the mind;
Which make the fpirit mount on high,
    And leave the world behind.

6. No more, believers, mourn your lot,
    But if you are the Lord's,
Refign to them that know him not,
    Such joys as earth affords.

HYMN XXIV.

Queen of Sheba.

1. FROM Sheba a diftant report
    Of Solomon's glory and fame,
Invited the Queen to his court,
    But all was outdone when fhe came;
She cry'd with a pleafing furprize,
    When firft fhe before him appear'd,
" How much, what I fee with my eyes,
" Surpaffes the rumor I heard."

2. When once to Jerufalem come,
    The treafure and train fhe had brought,
The wealth fhe poffeffed at home,
    No longer had place in her thought:
His houfe, *his* attendants, *his* throne,
    All ftruck her with wonder and awe;
The glory of Solomon fhone,
    In every object fhe faw.

3. But Solomon moft fhe admir'd,
    Whofe fpirit conducted the whole;
His wifdom, which God had infpir'd,
    His bounty and greatnefs of foul;

Of all the hard queſtions ſhe put,
  A ready ſolution he ſhew'd;
Exceeded her wiſh and her ſuit,
  And more than ſhe aſk'd him beſtow'd.

. Thus I when the goſpel proclaim'd
  The Saviour's great name in my ears,
The wiſdom for which he is fam'd,
  The love which to ſinners he bears;
I long'd, and I was not deny'd,
  That I in his preſence might bow;
I ſaw, and tranſported I cry'd,
  " A greater than Solomon Thou!"

. My conſcience no comfort could find,
  By doubt and hard queſtions oppos'd;
But he reſtor'd peace to my mind,
  And anſwer'd each doubt I propos'd!
Beholding me poor and diſtreſs'd,
  His bounty ſupply'd all my wants;
My pray'r could have never expreſs'd
  So much as this Solomon grants.

. I heard, and was ſlow to believe,
  But now with my eyes I behold,
Much more than my heart could conceive,
  Or language could ever have told:
How happy thy ſervants muſt be,
  Who always before thee appear!
Vouchſafe, Lord, this bleſſing to me,
  I find it is good to be here.

HYMN

HYMN XXV.

The pool of Bethesda.

1. BESIDE the gospel pool
    Appointed for the poor;
  From year to year, my helpless soul
    Has waited for a cure.

2. How often have I seen
    The healing waters move!
  And others, round me, stepping in
    Their efficacy prove!

3. But my complaints remain,
    I feel the very same:
  As full of guilt, and fear, and pain,
    As when at first I came,

4. O would the Lord appear
    My malady to heal!
  He knows how long I've languish'd here,
    And what distress I feel.

5. How often have I thought
    Why should I longer lie?
  Surely the mercy I have sought
    Is not for such as I.

6. But whether can I go?
    There is no other pool

Where

Where streams of sov'reign virtue flow
  To make a sinner whole.

7. Here then, from day to day,
  I'll wait, and hope, and try;
Can Jesus hear a sinner pray,
  Yet suffer him to die?

8. No: He is full of grace;
  He never will permit
A soul, that fain would see his face,
  To perish at his feet.

HYMN XXVI.

1. GRACIOUS Lord, incline thine ear,
  My complaint vouchsafe to hear;
Sore distrest with guilt am I,
Give me Christ, or else I die.

2. Wealth and honour I disdain,
Earthly comforts all are vain;
They can never satisfy,
Give me Christ, or else I die.

3. Lord deny me what thou wilt,
Only take away my guilt;
Mourning at thy feet I lie;
Give me Christ, or else I die.

4. All unholy and unclean,
I am sinful, vile and mean;

But

But to thee for mercy fly,
Give me Chrift or elfe I die.

5. Thou doft freely fave the loft;
In thy grace alone I truft:
Unto thee I lift my cry,
Give me Chrift, or elfe I die.

6. O my God, what fhall I fay?
Take, oh take my fins away!
Jefu's blood to me apply,
Give me Chrift, or elfe I die.

HYMN XXVII.

The Difciples at fea.

1. COnftrain'd by their Lord to embark,
    And venture without him to fea;
The feafon tempeftuous and dark,
    How griev'd the difciples muft be!
But tho' he remain'd on the fhore,
    He fpent the night for them in pray'r;
They ftill were as fafe as before,
    And equally under his care.

2. They ftrove, tho' in vain, for a while,
    The force of the waves to withftand;
But when they were weary'd with toil,
    They faw their dear Saviour at hand;
They gladly receiv'd him on board,
    His prefence their fpirits reviv'd;

The

The sea became calm at his word,
   And soon at their port they arriv'd.

3. Believers now like them are tost
   By storms, on a perilous deep;
But cannot be possibly lost
   While Jesus has charge of the ship:
Tho' billows and winds are enrag'd,
   And threaten to make them their sport;
This Pilot hath firmly engag'd
   To bring them, in safety, to port.

4. If sometimes we struggle alone,
   And he is withdrawn from our view,
It makes us more willing to own
   We nothing, without him, can do:
Then Satan our hopes would assail,
   But Jesus is still within call;
And when our poor efforts quite fail,
   He comes in good time, and does all.

5. Yet, Lord, we are ready to shrink
   Unless we thy presence perceive;
O save us (we cry) or we sink,
   We would, but we cannot believe:
The night has been long and severe,
   The winds and the seas are still high;
Dear Saviour, this moment appear,
   And say to our souls, "It is I!".

HYMN XXVIII.

The foolish Virgins.

1. WHEN descending from the sky
    The Bridegroom shall appear;
 And the solemn midnight cry,
    Shall call professors near;
 How the sound our hearts will damp!
    How will shame o'erspread each face!
 If we only have a lamp,
    Without the oil of grace.

2. Foolish virgins then will wake,
    And seek for a supply;
 But in vain the pains they take
    To borrow or to buy:
 Then with those they now despise,
    Earnestly they'll wish to share;
 But the best among the wise,
    Will have no oil to spare.

3. Wise are they, and truly blest,
    Who then shall ready be!
 But despair will seize the rest,
    And dreadful misery:
 " Once, they'll cry, we scorn'd to doubt,
    " Tho' in lies our trust we put;
 " Now our lamp of hope is out,
    " The door of mercy shut."

4. If they then prefume to plead,
   "Lord, open to us now;
"We on earth have heard and pray'd,
   "And with thy faints did bow:"
He will anfwer from his throne,
   "Tho' you with my people mix'd,
"Yet to me you ne'er were known,
   "Depart, your doom is fix'd."

5. O that none who worfhip here
   May hear that word, Depart!
Lord imprefs a godly fear
   On each profeffor's heart:
Help us, Lord, to fearch the camp,
   Let us not ourfelves beguile;
Trufting to a dying lamp
   Without a ftock of oil.

HYMN XXIX.

The two Debtors.

1. ONCE a woman filent ftood
      While Jefus fat at meat;
From her eyes fhe pour'd a flood
   To wafh his facred feet:
Shame and wonder, joy and love,
   All at once poffefs'd her mind,
That fhe ere fo vile could prove,
   Yet now forgivenefs find.

2. "How came this vile woman here?
   "Will Jefus notice fuch?

D 2

"Sure,

" Sure, if he a prophet were,
　" He would difdain her touch!"
Simon thus, with fcornful heart,
　Slighted one whom Jefus lov'd;
But her Saviour took her part,
　And thus his pride reprov'd:

3. " If two men in debt were bound,
　" One lefs, the other more;
" Fifty, or five hundred pound,
　" And both alike were poor;
" Should the lender both forgive,
　" When he faw them both diftrefs'd;
" Which of them would you believe
　" Engag'd to love him beft?

4. " Surely he who moft did owe,"
　The Pharifee reply'd;
Then our Lord, " By judging fo,
　" Thou doft for her decide:
" Simon, if like her you knew
　" How much you forgivenefs need;
" You like her had acted too,
　" And welcom'd me indeed!

5. " When the load of fin is felt,
　" And much forgivenefs known;
" Then the heart of courfe will melt,
　" Tho' hard before as ftone:
" Blame not then her love and tears,
　" Greatly fhe in debt has been;
" But I have remov'd her fears,
　" And pardon'd all her fin."

　　　　　　　　　　6. When

6. When I read this woman's case,
   Her love and humble zeal;
I confess, with shame of face,
   My heart is made of steel:
Much has been forgiv'n to me,
   Jesus paid my heavy score;
What a creature must I be,
   That I can love no more!

HYMN XXX.

The Believer's Safety.

1. THAT man no guard or weapon needs,
      Whose heart the blood of Jesus knows;
   But safe may pass, if duty leads,
      Thro' burning sands or mountain-snows.

2. Releas'd from guilt he feels no fear,
      Redemption is his shield and tow'r;
   He sees his Saviour always near
      To help, in ev'ry trying hour.

3. Tho' I am weak, and Satan strong,
      And often to assault me tries;
   When Jesus is my shield and song,
      Abash'd the wolf before me flies.

4. His love possessing, I am blest,
      Secure whatever change may come;
   Whither I go to East or West,
      With him I still shall be at home.

5. If plac'd beneath the northern pole,
   Tho' winter reigns with vigor there;
His gracious beams would cheer my soul,
   And make a spring throughout the year.

6. Or if the defart's sun-burnt foil,
   My lonely dwelling e'er should prove,
His presence would support my toil,
   Whose smile is life, whose voice is love.

HYMN XXXI.

On one stone shall be seven eyes.

1. JESUS CHRIST, the Lord's anointed,
      Who his blood for sinners spilt;
   Is the stone by God appointed,
      And the church is on him built:
         He delivers
      All who trust him from their guilt.

2. Many eyes at once are fixed
      On a person so divine;
   Love, with awful justice mixed,
      In his great redemption shine:
         Mighty Jesus!
      Give me leave to call thee mine.

3. By the Father's eye approved,
      Lo, a voice is heard from Heav'n,
   " Sinners, this is my Beloved,
      " For your ransom freely giv'n:
         " All offences,
      " For his sake shall be forgiv'n."

4. An-

4. Angels with their eyes purfu'd him,
   When he left his glorious throne;
With aftonifhment they view'd him,
   Put the form of fervant on:
      Angels worfhipp'd
   Him who was on earth unknown.

5. Satan and his hoft amazed,
   Saw this ftone in Zion laid;
Jefus, tho' to death abafed,
   Bruis'd the fubtil ferpent's head:
      When to fave us,
   On the crofs his blood he fhed.

6. When a guilty finner fees him,
   While he looks his foul is heal'd;
Soon this fight from anguifh frees him,
   And imparts a pardon feal'd:
      May this Saviour
   Be to all our hearts reveal'd!

7. With defire and admiration,
   All his blood bought flock behold
Him, who wrought out their falvation,
   And enclos'd them in his fold:
      Yet their warmeft
   Love and praifes are too cold.

8. By the eye of carnal reafon
   Many view him with difdain;
How will they abide the feafon
   When he'll come with all his train?
      To efcape him
   Then they'll wifh, but wifh in vain.

9. How

9. How their hearts will melt and tremble
   When they hear his awful voice!
But his saints he'll then assemble,
   As his portion, and his choice:
      And receive them
   To his everlasting joys.

HYMN XXXII.

New year's day.

1. NOW, gracious Lord, thine arm reveal,
      And make thy glory known;
   Now let us all thy presence feel,
      And soften hearts of stone!

2. Help us to venture near thy throne,
      And plead a Saviour's name;
   For all that we can call our own,
      Is vanity and shame.

3. From all the guilt of former sin
      May mercy set us free;
   And let the year we now begin,
      Begin and end with thee.

4. Send down thy Spirit from above,
      That saints may love thee more;
   And sinners now may learn to love
      Who never lov'd before.

5. And when before thee we appear
      In our eternal home;
   May growing numbers worship here,
      And praise thee in our room.

HYMN

HYMN XXXIII.

1. BESTOW, dear Lord, upon our youth
    The gift of saving grace;
And let the seed of sacred truth
    Fall in a fruitful place.

2. Grace is a plant, where'er it grows,
    Of pure and heav'nly root;
But fairest in the youngest shews,
    And yields the sweetest fruit.

3. Ye careless ones, O hear betimes
    The voice of sov'reign love!
Your youth is stain'd with many crimes,
    But mercy reigns above.

4. True, you are young, but there's a stone
    Within the youngest breast;
Or half the crimes which you have done
    Would rob you of your rest.

5. For you the public pray'r is made,
    Oh! join the public pray'r!
For you the secret tear is shed,
    O shed yourselves a tear!

6. We pray that you may early prove
    The Spirit's pow'r to teach:
You cannot be too young to love
    That Jesus whom we preach.

HYMN XXXIV.

1. WHEN Paul was parted from his friends
    It was a weeping day;
But Jesus made them all amends,
    And wip'd their tears away.

2. Ere long they met again with joy,
    (Secure no more to part.)
Where praises ev'ry tongue employ,
    And pleasure fills each heart.

3. Thus all the preachers of his grace
    Their children soon shall meet;
Together see their Saviour's face,
    And worship at his feet.

4. But they who heard the word in vain,
    Tho' oft and plainly warn'd;
Will tremble when they meet again
    The ministers they scorn'd.

5. On your own heads your blood will fall,
    If any perish here;
The preachers, who have told you *all*,
    Shall stand approv'd, and clear.

6. Yet, Lord, to save themselves alone,
    Is not their utmost view;
Oh! hear their pray'r, thy message own,
    And save their hearers too.

HYMN XXXV. *Paul's voyage.*

1. IF Paul in Cæsar's court must stand,
    He need not fear the sea;
  Secur'd from harm, on ev'ry hand,
    By the divine decree.

2. Altho' the ship wherein he sail'd,
    By dreadful storms was toss'd;
  The promise over all prevail'd,
    And not a life was lost.

3. Jesus! the God whom Paul ador'd,
    Who saves in time of need;
  Was then confess'd by all on board,
    A present help indeed!

4. Tho' neither sun nor stars were seen
    Paul knew the Lord was near;
  And faith preserv'd his soul serene,
    When others shook with fear.

5. Believers thus are toss'd about
    On life's tempestuous main;
  But grace assures beyond a doubt
    They shall their port attain.

6. They must, they shall appear one day,
    Before their Saviour's throne;
  The storms they meet with by the way,
    But make his power known.

7. Their

7. Their paſſage lies acroſs the brink
    Of many a threat'ning wave;
The world expects to ſee them ſink,
    But Jeſus lives to ſave.

8. Lord, tho' we are but feeble worms,
    Yet ſince thy word is paſt;
We'll venture thro' a thouſand ſtorms,
    To ſee thy face at laſt.

HYMN XXXVI.

The day of judgment.

1. DAY of judgment, day of wonders!
      Hark! the trumpet's awful ſound,
Louder than a thouſand thunders,
      Shakes the vaſt creation round!
        How the ſummons
      Will the ſinner's heart confound!

2. See the judge our nature wearing,
      Cloth'd in majeſty divine!
You who long for his appearing,
      Then ſhall ſay, " This God is mine!"
        Gracious Saviour,
      Own me in that day for thine!

3. At his call the dead awaken,
      Riſe to life from earth and ſea;
All the pow'rs of nature then
      By his look, prepare to flee:

Care-

Carelefs finner,
What will then become of thee?

4. Horrors paſt imagination,
   Will furprize your trembling heart,
When you hear your condemnation,
   " Hence, accurfed wretch, depart!
   " Thou with Satan
   " And his Angels, have thy part!"

5. Satan, who now tries to pleafe you,
   Left you timely warning take,
When that word is paſt, will feize you,
   Plunge you in the burning lake:
   Think, poor finner,
   Thy eternal all's at ſtake!

6. But to thofe who have confeſſed,
   Lov'd and ferv'd the Lord below;
He will fay, " Come near ye bleſſed,
   " See the kingdom I beſtow:
   " You for ever
   " Shall my love and glory know."

7. Under forrows and reproaches,
   May this thought your courage raife!
Swiftly God's great day approaches,
   Sighs fhall then be chang'd to praife:
   We fhall triumph
   When the world is in a blaze.

E   HYMN

HYMN XXXVII.

The Good that I would I do not.

1. I Would but cannot sing,
    Guilt has untun'd my voice;
  The Serpent sin's envenom'd sting
    Has poison'd all my joys.

2. I know the Lord is nigh,
    And would, but cannot pray;
  For Satan meets me when I try,
    And frights my soul away.

3. I would, but can't repent
    Tho' I endeavour oft;
  This stony heart can ne'er relent
    'Till Jesus makes it soft.

4. I would, but cannot love,
    Tho' woo'd by love Divine;
  No arguments have pow'r to move
    A soul so base as mine.

5. I would, but cannot rest
    In God's most holy will;
  I know what He appoints is best,
    Yet murmur at it still.

6. Oh could I but believe!
    Then all would easy be;
  I would, but cannot; Lord relieve,
    My help must come from thee!

7. But

7. But if indeed I *wou'd*,
   Tho' I can nothing do;
Yet the desire is something good,
   For which my praise is due.

8. By nature prone to ill,
   Till thine appointed hour
I was as destitute of will,
   As now I am of pow'r.

9. Wilt thou not crown, at length,
   The work thou hast begun?
And with a will, afford me strength
   In all thy ways to run.

HYMN XXXVIII.

1. I'VE found the Pearl of greatest price,
      My heart doth sing for joy:
   And sing I must, a Christ I have;
      O what a Christ have I?

2. Christ is the Way, the Truth, the Life,
      The Way to God on high,
   Life to the dead, the Truth of Types,
      The Truth of Prophesy.

3. Christ is a Prophet, Priest and King:
      A Prophet full of light,
   A Priest that stands 'twixt God and man,
      A King that rules with might.

4. Christ's

4. Chrift's Manhood is a Temple, where
    The Altar God doth reft;
My Chrift, he is the Sacrifice,
    My Chrift he is the Prieft.

5. My Chrift he is the Lord of Lords,
    He is the King of Kings;
He is the Sun of Righteoufnefs,
    With Healing in his Wings.

6. My Chrift, he is the Tree of life,
    Which in God's garden grows;
Whofe Fruit does feed, whofe Leaves do heal:
    My Chrift is Sharon's Rofe.

7. Chrift is my Meat, Chrift is my Drink,
    My Phyfick and my Health,
My Peace, my Strength, my Joy, my Crown,
    My Glory and my Wealth.

8. Chrift is my Father, and my Friend,
    My Brother and my Love;
My Head, my Hope, my Counfellor,
    My Advocate above.

9. My Chrift, he is the Heav'n of Heav'ns,
    My Chrift what fhall I call?
My Chrift is Firft, my Chrift is laft,
    My Chrift is All in All.

HYMN

HYMN XXXIX.

1 Bright burning beams of gofpel grace
   Hafte Lord, for to difplay;
For to burn up in all thy faints
   Their ftubble, wood, and hay.

2. Break forth O Sun of Righteoufnefs
   Unto the perfect day:
Hafte Holy One unto thy throne,
   Our Jefus, hafte away!

3. But O, who may abide the day
   When Zion's King fhall reign?
Who may abide, when he the pride
   Of all proud flefh fhall ftain?

4. Tremble ye carelefs ones, that are
   At eafe in Zion, and
Wonder and ftay, becaufe that day
   Is very nigh at hand:

5. It now doth dawn; the glorious morn
   Begins for to appear;
What elfe do mean thefe lowings, and
   Thefe bleatings we do hear?

6. The faints do fing to Chrift their King,
   Whilft others rage in pain,
Becaufe His bright and dazzling Light
   Shines thro' the world amain.

7. Re-

7. Redeemed ones, sing praises, for
This fire's but sent to try,
And purge your dross, that by its loss
Christ may you purify.

HYMN XL.

1. LORD, thou hast planted me a vine
In fertile soil and air;
Now tend and water me as thine,
And make me still thy care.

2. My Christ I'm wholly thine, direct
My goings, for I'm dark;
O may my constant aims be right!
Thine honor be my mark!

3. Shall Simon bear thy cross alone,
And other saints be free?
Each saint of thine shall find his own,
And there is one for me:

4. Whene'er it falls unto my lot,
Let it not frighten me;
Nor drive me from my gracious God,
But bring me home to thee.

5. O happy Christians, be not loth
To have a coarser fare;
Saints that have had no table-cloth
Had Christ at dinner there.

6. To

6. To do or suffer I am pleas'd,
   So long as Christ stands by;
Support me with thy constant aid,
   Lest all thy graces die.

7. Thy way is to the upright strength;
   Lord, make it so to me,
That never tiring with the length,
   My soul may reach to thee.

HYMN XLI.

Lamenting the Loss of First Love.

1. O That my soul were now as fair
      As it hath sometimes been!
   Devoid of that distracting care
      Without, and fear within!

2. There was a time when I could tread
      No circle but of love:
   That joyous morning now is fled,
      How heavily I move!

3. Unhappy soul, that thou should'st force
      Thy Saviour to depart,
   When he was pleased with so coarse
      A lodging in thy heart!

4. How sweetly I enjoy'd my God!
      With how divine a frame!
   I thought, on ev'ry plant I trod,
      I read my Saviour's name;

5. I liv'd, I lov'd, I talk'd with thee,
    So fweetly we agreed,
And thou no ftranger waft to me
    Till I became a weed.

6. The tempter robb'd me, and I muft
    I fear be ever poor;
May this fuffice, to roll in duft
    Before thy temple door!

7. My deareft Lord, my heart flames not
    With love, that facred fire;
But fince my love has wore that blot
    Repentance runs the high'r.

8. O might thofe days return again,
    How welcome they fhould be!
Shall my petition be in vain,
    Since grace is ever free?

9. Lord of my foul, return, return,
    To chafe away this night;
Let not thine anger ever burn;
    God once was my delight.

H Y M N   XLII.

1. MY Lord, my God, I once could fing
    But now I fear to fay
My God; I only cry my King,
    Of force I muft obey.

2. I've

2. I've forfeited that blessed Guest,
   That joy that sometimes shone
Within this dark unhallow'd breast;
   O whither is it gone?

3. In infinite compassion Lord,
   To my complaint give ear;
Whole troops of sorrows bear me down;
   O when wilt thou appear?

4. Remember, Lord, what I am stil'd,
   Tho' under darkness great;
Tho' under darkness, still thy child,
   My heart is still thy seat.

5. My King, thou dost possess that throne,
   Thou dost that sceptre sway;
'Tis thine, still, Lord, 'tis thine alone,
   I hate the sinner's way:

6. Lord, when thou seest me come to pray,
   Bow down a gracious ear
To answer; if my Lord delay,
   One darksome day's a year.

7. To shine upon a soul so vile,
   Would magnify thy grace;
I long for nothing but a smile
   From my dear Saviour's face.

8. I will no more my Lord provoke,
   Or cause thee to withdraw,

Thy

Thy former frowns have made me wife,
  To fear, and stand in awe.

9. My restless soul will ne'er give o'er,
  Until thy bowels move;
I'll not be driven from thy door
  Till thou shalt say, " I love."

HYMN XLIII.

1. ALAS, my God, that thou should be
  To me so much unknown!
I long to walk and talk with Thee,
  And dwell before thy throne.

2. Thou know'st, my soul does dearly love
  The place of thine abode;
No music gives so sweet a sound,
  As these two words, *My God*.

3. I long not for the fruit that grows
  Within these gardens here;
I find no sweetness in their rose
  When Jesus is not near.

4. Thy gracious Presence, O my Christ,
  Can make a Paradise;
Ah, what are all the goodly pearls,
  Unto this Pearl of price?

5. Give me that sweet communion, Lord,
  Thy people have with thee;

Thy Spirit daily talks with them,
  O let it talk with me.

6. Like Enoch let me walk with God,
    And thus walk out my day,
Attended with the heav'nly guards,
    Upon the King's high way.

7. When wilt thou come unto me, Lord?
    O come, my Lord, moſt dear;
Come near, come nearer, nearer ſtill;
    I'm well when thou art near.

8. When wilt thou come unto me, Lord?
    I languiſh for thy ſight;
Ten thouſand Suns, if thou art ſtrange,
    Are ſhades inſtead of light.

9. When wilt thou come unto me, Lord?
    For till thou doſt appear,
I count each moment for a day,
    Each minute for a year.

10. Come, Lord, and never from me go,
    This world's a darkſome place;
I find no pleaſure here below,
    When thou doſt veil thy face.

11. There's no ſuch thing as pleaſure here,
    My Jeſus is my all;
As thou doſt ſhine, or diſappear,
    My pleaſures riſe and fall.

12. Come

12. Come spread thy Savour on my frame,
   No sweetness is so sweet;
Till I get up to sing thy name,
   Where all thy singers meet.

HYMN XLIV.

1. O, Was I first born from beneath;
      And then born from above!
   Am I a child of man and God?
      O rich and endless love!

2. Earth is my mother, earth my nurse,
      And earth must be my tomb:
   Yet God, the God of Heav'n and Earth,
      My Father is become.

3. Hell enter'd me, and into hell
      I quickly should have run;
   But O! kind Heav'n laid hold on me;
      Heav'n is in me begun.

4. This spark will rise into a flame,
      This seed into a tree;
   My songs shall rise, my praises shall
      Loud Hallelujah's be.

HYMN XLV.

1. I That am drawn out of the depth,
      Will sing upon the shore:
   I that in hell's dark suburbs lay,
      Pure mercy will adore.

2. The

2. The terrors of the living God
    My foul did fo affright;
I fear'd left I fhould be condemn'd
    To an eternal night.

3. Kind was the pity of my friends,
    But could not eafe my fmart;
Their words indeed did reach my cafe,
    But could not reach my heart.

4. Ah, what was then this world to me,
    To whom God's word was dark?
Who in my dungeon could not fee
    One beam or fhining fpark!

5. What then were all the creatures fmiles,
    When the Creator frown'd?
My days were nights, my life was death,
    My being was my wound.

6. Tortur'd and rack'd, with hellifh fears,
    Left God the blow fhould give;
Mine eyes did fail, my heart did fink
    Then mercy bid me live.

HYMN XLVI.

1. LORD of my life, length of my days,
    Thy hand hath refcu'd me;
Who lying at the gates of death
    Among the dead was free.

2. My dearest friends I had resign'd
    Unto their Maker's care;
Methought I only time had left
    For a concluding pray'r.

3. Methought death laid his hand on me,
    And did his pris'ner bind;
And by the sound, methought I heard
    His Master's feet behind.

4. Methought I stood upon the shore,
    And nothing could I see,
But the vast Ocean with my eyes,
    A vast Eternity.

5. Methought I heard the midnight cry,
    Behold the Bridegroom comes:
Methought he call'd me to his bar,
    Where souls receive their dooms.

6. The world was at an end to me,
    As if it all did burn;
But lo! there came a voice of pow'r,
    Which order'd my return.

7. Lord, I return'd at thy command,
    What wilt thou have me do?
O let me wholly live to thee,
    To whom my life I owe.

8. Fain would I dedicate to thee
    The remnant of my days:

Lord, with my life renew my heart,
That both thy name may praise.

HYMN XLVII.

Christ the Beloved described.

1. FAIR Salem's daughters aſk to know
    Why I ſhould love my Jeſus ſo;
What are his charms, ſay they, *above*
The objects of another's love?

2. Yes, my Beloved, to my ſight
    Shews a ſweet mixture, red and white;
All human beauties, all divine,
    In my Beloved meet and ſhine.

3. White is his ſoul, from blemiſh free;
    Red with the blood he ſhed for me;
The Faireſt of ten thouſand fairs;
    A Sun among ten thouſand ſtars.

4. His head the fineſt gold excels;
    There wiſdom in perfection dwells,
And glory, like a crown, adorns
    Thoſe temples once beſet with thorns.

5. Compaſſions in his heart are found,
    Hard by the ſignals of his wound:
His ſacred ſide no more ſhall bear
    The cruel ſcourge, the piercing ſpear.

6. His

6. His hands are fairer to behold
    Than diamonds fet in rings of gold;
Thofe heav'nly hands that on the tree
    Were nail'd, and torn, and bled for me.

7. Tho' once he bow'd his feeble knees,
    Loaded with fins and agonies,
Now on the throne of his command,
    His legs like marble pillars ftand.

8. His eyes are majefty and love,
    The eagle temper'd with the dove;
No more fhall trickling forrows roll,
    Thro' thofe dear windows of his foul.

9. His mouth that pour'd out long complaints,
    Now fmiles, and cheers his fainting faints:
His countenance more graceful is
    Than Lebanon with all its trees.

10. All over glorious is my Lord,
    Muft be belov'd, and yet ador'd;
His worth if all the nations knew,
    Sure ev'ry one would love him too.

HYMN XLVIII.

1. WHILE thus my deareft Love I prais'd,
        As I could do no lefs,
They heard, they look'd, they ftood amaz'd
    At my great happinefs.

2. And

2. And when I ceas'd, they thus reply'd,
  " O fairest, we must needs
" Congratulate thy blest estate,
  " Which ours so far exceeds.

3. " O that we were in such a case
  " As we perceive thou art!
" O that our souls might find a place
  " In thy Beloved's heart!

4. " Whither is thy Beloved gone?
  " Pray let us go with thee,
" To seek thy well beloved one,
  " Whose face we fain would see."

5. If you my dearest Lord would see,
  Then go into his court;
Look where his saints assembled be,
  Thither you must resort.

6. For they his pleasure gardens are,
  Where he delights to be;
They are his comfort and his care,
  There you my Lord may see.

7. Some souls he breeds, and some he feeds,
  Others he doth remove
Hence from his lower gardens, to
  His paradise above.

8. I am my well Beloved's own,
  My well Beloved's mine:

To me his love a feast doth prove
  Beyond the richest wine.

HYMN XLIX.

1. ARISE, O King of grace, arise,
    And enter to thy rest;
  Lo thy church waits with longing eyes,
    Thus to be own'd and blest.

2. Enter with all thy glorious train,
    Thy Spirit and thy word;
  All that the Ark did once contain
    Could no such grace afford.

3. Here mighty God, accept our vows,
    Here let thy praise be spread,
  Bless the provisions of thy house,
    And fill thy poor with bread.

4. Here let the Son of David reign,
    Let God's anointed shine;
  Justice and truth his court maintain,
    With love and pow'r divine.

5. Here let him hold a lasting throne,
    And as his kingdom grows,
  Fresh honours shall adorn his crown,
    And shame confound his foes.

HYMN

HYMN L.

1. JESUS, the only thought of thee,
  With sweetness fills my breast;
But sweeter far it is to see,
  And on thy beauty feast.

2. No sound, no harmony so gay,
  Can art of music frame;
No thoughts can reach, no words can say
  The sweets of thy blest name.

3. Jesus, our hope, when we repent,
  Sweet source of all our grace;
Sole comfort in our banishment,
  O! what when face to face!

4. Jesus! that name inspires my mind
  With springs of life and light;
More than I ask in thee I find,
  And lavish in delight.

5. No art, or eloquence of man,
  Can tell the joys of love;
Only the saints can understand
  What they in Jesus prove.

6. Thee then I'll seek retir'd apart,
  From world and business free;
When these shall knock, I'll shut my heart,
  And keep it all for thee.

7. Be

7. Before the morning light I'll come,
　　With Magdalene, to find,
In sighs and tears, my Jesu's tomb,
　　And there refresh my mind.

8. My tears upon his grave shall flow,
　　My sighs the garden fill;
Then at his feet myself I'll throw,
　　And there I'll seek his will.

9. Jesus, in thy bless'd steps I'll tread,
　　And walk in all thy ways;
I'll never cease to weep and plead,
　　Till I'm restor'd to grace.

10. O King of Love, thy blessed fire
　　Does such sweet flames excite;
That first it raises our desire
　　Then fills us with delight.

11. Thy lovely presence shines so clear
　　Thro' every sense and way,
That souls which once have seen thee near,
　　See all things else decay.

12. Come then, dear Lord, possess my heart,
　　Chase thence the shades of night;
Come pierce it with thy flaming dart,
　　And ever-shining light.

13. Then I'll for ever Jesus sing,
　　And with the saints rejoice;
And both my heart and tongue shall bring
Their tribute to my dearest King,
　　In never-ending joys.　Amen.

HYMN

HYMN LI.

1. TWO are better far than one
    For counsel or for fight;
How can one be warm alone?
    Or serve his God aright?
Join we then our hearts and hands:
    Each to love provoke his friend;
Run the way of his commands,
    And keep it to the end.

2. Woe to him whose spirits droop!
    To him who falls alone!
He has none to lift him up,
    To help his weakness on:
Happier we each other keep;
    We each others burdens bear;
Never need our footsteps slip,
    Upheld by mutual pray'r.

3. Who of twain has made us one,
    Maintains our unity:
Jesus is the corner stone,
    In whom we all agree:
Servants of one common Lord,
    Sweetly of one heart and mind,
Who can break a threefold cord
    Or part whom God hath join'd?

4. Oh that all with us might prove
    The fellowship of saints!
And supply'd in Jesu's love
    What ev'ry member wants!

Grasp

Grasp we our high callings prize!
   Feel our sins on earth forgiv'n!
Rise, in his whole image rise,
   And meet our head in heav'n!

HYMN LII.

1. LORD; I believe a rest remains
   To all thy people known,
A rest where pure enjoyment reigns,
   And thou art lov'd alone.

2. A rest where all our souls desire
   Is fixt on things above;
Where fear and sin, and grief expire,
   Cast out by perfect love.

3. Oh that I now the rest might know,
   Believe, and enter in!
Now Saviour, now the pow'r bestow,
   And let me cease from sin!

4. Remove this hardness from my heart,
   This unbelief remove:
To me the rest of faith impart,
   The sabbath of thy love.

5. I would be thine; thou know'st I would,
   And have thee all my own:
Thee, Oh! my all-sufficient good,
   I want, and thee alone.

6. Thy

6. Thy name to me, thy nature grant!
   This, only this, be giv'n:
Nothing beside my God I want,
   Nothing in earth or heav'n.

7. Come, Oh my Saviour, come away,
   Into my soul descend!
No longer from thy creature stay,
   My author and my end!

8. Come, Father, Son, and Holy Ghost,
   And seal me thine abode!
Let all I am in thee be lost,
   Let all be lost in God.

HYMN LIII.

1. MESSIAH, full of grace
      Redeem'd by thee we plead
   The promise made to Abra'ms race
      To souls for ages dead.

2. Their bones as quite dry'd up
      Throughout the vale appear;
   Cut off and lost their last faint hope
      To see thy kingdom here.

3. Open their graves, and bring
      The outcasts forth to own
   Thou art their Lord, their God and King,
      Their true anointed one.

4. To fave the race forlorn
   Thy glorious arm difplay:
And fhew the world a nation born,
   A nation in a day!

HYMN LIV.

1. FATHER of faithful Abra'm, hear,
      Our earneſt ſuit for Abra'ms feed!
Juſtly they claim the fofteſt pray'r
   From us, adopted in their ſtead:
Who mercy through their fall obtain,
And Chriſt by their rejection gain.

2. Outcaſts from thee and ſcatter'd wide
      Through ev'ry nation under heav'n
Blafpheming whom they crucify'd,
   Unfav'd, unpity'd, unforgiv'n.
Branded like Cain, they bear their load,
Abhorr'd of men, and curs'd of God.

3. But haſt thou finally forfook,
      Forever caſt thy own away?
Wilt thou not bid the murd'rers look
   On him they pierc'd, and weep and pray?
Yes gracious Lord, thy word is paſt:
All Iſrael ſhall be fav'd at laſt.

4. Come then, thou great deliv'rer come!
      The veil from Jacob's heart remove!
Receive thy ancient people home;
   That quicken'd by thy dying love,

The

The world may their reception find,
Life from the dead for all mankind.

HYMN LV.

1. HOLY Lamb, who thee receive,
Who in thee begin to live,
Day and night they cry to thee,
As thou art, so let us be!

2. Jesu, see my panting breast:
See I pant in thee to rest!
Gladly would I now be clean:
Cleanse me now from ev'ry sin.

3. Fix, Oh! fix my wav'ring mind;
To thy cross my spirit bind;
Earthly passions far remove;
Swallow up our souls in love.

4. Dust and ashes though we be,
Full of guilt and misery,
Thine we are, thou Son of God:
Take the purchase of thy blood!

5. Who in heart on thee believes,
He th' atonement now receives:
He with joy beholds thy face
Triumphs in thy pard'ning grace.

6. See ye sinners, see the flame
Rising from the slaughter'd Lamb;
Marks the new, the living way,
Leading to eternal day!

7. Jesu,

7. Jesu, when this light we see,
All our soul's athirst for thee:
When thy quick'ning pow'r we prove,
All our heart dissolves in love.

8. Boundless wisdom, pow'r divine,
Love unspeakable are thine!
Praise by all to thee be giv'n
Sons of earth, and hosts of heav'n.

HYMN LVI.

1. LET Christ the glorious lover
   Have everlasting praise;
He cometh to discover
   The riches of his grace:
He courts the wretched sinner,
   To be his loving bride;
Resolving for to win her,
   And will not be deny'd.

2. When first he calls upon her,
   Herself for to deny,
To cast away her honour,
   And lay her pleasures by,
To part with ev'ry notion
   That puft her up with pride,
And take him for her portion,
   And be his loving bride;

3. The offers he makes to her
   Are what she can't endure,

She thinks it will undo her
    To part with all her store;
She readily refuses
    To yield unto his will;
And in her heart she chuses
    Her former lovers still.

4. But when she is enlighten'd,
    Her conscience being stirr'd,
Her guilty soul is frighten'd,
    By his convincing word;
Then to escape his fury
    She now will take some pains,
And to obtain that glory
    Which ev'ry conqu'ror gains

5. She'll leave her ways of sinning,
    And read, and hear, and pray,
And think she is beginning
    To walk the narrow way:
She does not yet discover
    The filth of her inside,
But thinks the Lord will love her,
    And she shall be his bride.

6. But he displays his power,
    And shows the flaming sword,
With threat'nings to devour,
    He makes her hear his word;
She reads and feels salvation,
    But conscience doth engage
To shew her condemnation,
    Almost in ev'ry page.

7. Her heart she doth discover;
 And cannot now expect
That Jesus Christ will love her,
 Whom once she did reject.
He strips her of her beauties,
 Of which before she brags,
And shews her works and duties
 Are but like filthy rags.

8. And now she is bewailing
 Her sad benighted state;
And ev'ry little failing
 Appears exceeding great;
Her sins like to a mountain
 Before her do arise,
And hide the cleansing fountain
 From her beclouded eyes.

9. Dark doleful apprehensions
 Now fill her heart within,
And all her best inventions
 Can't cleanse her soul from sin.
Her groans and bitter crying,
 Might be compar'd to one
Just at the point of dying;
 She cries, " Undone! undone!"

10. Her thoughts are in confusion,
 And ev'ry hope of life
Appears to her delusion;
 Thus she is fill'd with strife.
For since Christ has convinc'd her,
 She thinks she knows full well

That all things are againſt her,
  In heaven, earth, and hell.

11. She oftentimes is fearing
  Her race is run too far,
And not one ſtar appearing
  By night to comfort her.
Both Prieſt and Levite by her
  Do paſs, which works her grief;
There's nothing yet comes nigh her,
  To give her ſoul relief.

12. But Jeſus has compaſſion
  Still moving in his heart,
Intends to give ſalvation,
  And eaſe her of her ſmart;
One glimpſe of loving power
  Makes her forget her pain;
She cries, " O happy hour!
  Is Jeſus come again?

13. Will he whom I rejected
  Come down to me ſo low?
Good news, but unexpected!
  This hardly can be ſo.
But now ſhe cries more fervent,
  " Lord don't thy mercy hide;
" Mayn't one become thy ſervant,
  Unfit to be a bride?"

14. But now her fears are double,
  Leſt he depart again,

And leave her still in trouble,
   For ever to remain.
She cries, " O glorious Saviour !
   (And speaks with all her heart)
" Let not my base behaviour
" Provoke thee to depart."

15. The day of her espousals
   To Jesus now draws near;
His terms and sweet proposals
   Her soul doth long to hear:
Now the Almighty lover
   No longer doth forbear,
But comes for to discover
   His glorious beauty fair.

16. And at the time appointed,
   Kind Jesus shews his face;
His countenance is pleasing,
   Adorn'd with richest grace:
With smiles, and sweet compassion;
   And blood to wash her white:
He comes with free salvation;
   'Tis a reviving sight.

17. Let saints and holy angels
   Attend with list'ning ear.
Unto the happy marriage
   Which we ere long shall hear,
Betwixt the Prince of heaven
   And sinful heir of hell,
A match that's more uneven
   Than tongues or pens can tell.

18. The

18. The guests that are invited,
    Are cloath'd in bright array,
Exceedingly delighted,
    Upon this wedding day:
With joy in all their faces,
    And harps to praise their King,
Their shouts and hallelujahs
    In heav'n and earth do ring.

19. The terms are now proposed,
    And Jesus takes his bride;
He gives himself unto her,
    And all things else beside:
And she without repining,
    Consents unto his terms,
Most joyfully resigning
    Herself into his arms.

20. Her husband is her Maker,
    Who doth her soul embrace;
And makes her a partaker
    Of ev'ry needful grace.
The world which so bewitches
    All Adam's race beside,
Can't imitate the riches
    Which Jesus gives his bride.

21. Her soul with admiration
    Can think what Jesus bore,
To purchase her salvation,
    And make the blessing sure:
She hears how he was wounded,
    And sacrific'd for sin,

Left

Left she should be confounded
 For evermore therein.

22. All sin, and earthly treasure,
 All Satan's snares and lies,
And best of carnal pleasure
 Are loathsome in her eyes:
Her longing soul desires,
 With speed to be remov'd
To join the heav'nly choirs
 And see her best Belov'd.

H Y M N LVII.

Submission to Afflictive Providences.

1. NAKED as from the earth we came,
 And crept to life at first,
We to the earth return again,
 And mingle with our dust.

2. The dear delights we here enjoy,
 And fondly call our own,
Are but short favours borrow'd now,
 To be repaid anon.

3. 'Tis God that lifts our comforts high,
 Or sinks them in the grave;
He gives, and (blessed be his Name!)
 He takes but what he gave.

4. Peace,

4. Peace, all our angry paſſions then!
      Let each rebellious ſigh
Be ſilent at his Sov'reign Will,
      And ev'ry murmur die.

5. If ſmiling mercy crown our lives,
      Its praiſes ſhall be ſpread,
And we'll adore the juſtice too
      That ſtrikes our comforts dead.

H Y M N   LVIII.

Triumph over Death.

1. GREAT God, I own thy ſentence juſt;
      And nature muſt decay;
I yield my body to the duſt,
      To dwell with fellow-clay.

2. Yet faith may triumph o'er the graves,
      And trample on the tombs;
My Jeſus, my Redeemer lives,
      My God, my Saviour comes.

3. The mighty conqu'ror ſhall appear
      High on a Royal ſeat,
And death, the laſt of all his foes,
      Lie vanquiſh'd at his feet.

4. Tho' greedy worms devour my ſkin,
      And gnaw my waſting fleſh,

When

When God shall build my bones again,
   He'll clothe them all afresh:

5. Then shall I see thy lovely face
   With strong immortal eyes,
And feast upon thy unknown grace
   With pleasure and surprize.

HYMN LIX.

The Blessedness of Gospel-Times.

1. HOW beauteous are their Feet
      Who stand on Zion's hill!
   Who bring salvation on their tongues,
      And words of peace reveal!

2. How charming is their voice!
      How sweet the tidings are!
   " Zion, behold thy Saviour-King,
      " He reigns and triumphs here."

3. How happy are our ears
      That hear this joyful sound,
   Which kings and prophets waited for,
      And sought, but never found!

4. How blessed are our eyes
      That see this heav'nly Light;
   Prophets and kings desir'd it long,
      But dy'd without the sight!

5. The

5. The watchmen join their voice,
    And tuneful notes employ;
Jerusalem breaks forth in songs,
    And desarts learn the joy.

6. The Lord makes bare his arm
    Thro' all the earth abroad:
Let ev'ry nation now behold
    Their Saviour and their God.

HYMN LX.

A Vision of the Kingdom of Christ among Men.

1. LO, what a glorious sight appears
    To our believing eyes!
The earth and seas are pass'd away,
    And the old rolling skies:

2. From the third Heav'n, where God resides,
    That holy, happy place,
The new Jerusalem comes down,
    Adorn'd with shining grace.

3. Attending angels shout for joy,
    And the bright armies sing,
" Mortals, behold the sacred Seat
    " Of your descending King!

4. " The God of Glory down to men
    " Removes his bless'd abode;
                    " Men,

" Men, the dear objects of his Grace,
"   And He the loving God.

5. " His own soft Hand shall wipe the tears
"   From ev'ry weeping eye;
" And pains and groans, and griefs, and fears,
"   And death itself shall die."

6. How long, dear Saviour, O how long!
   Shall this bright hour delay?
Fly swiftly round, ye wheels of time,
   And bring the welcome day.

H Y M N   LXI.

Assurances of Heaven: or, a Saint prepar'd to die.

[1. DEATH may dissolve my body now,
      And bear my spirit home;
Why do my minutes move so slow,
   Nor my salvation come?

2. With heav'nly weapons I have fought
      The battles of the Lord,
Finish'd my course and kept the faith,
   And wait the sure reward.]

3. God has laid up in Heav'n for me
   A crown which cannot fade;
The Righteous Judge at that great day
   Shall place it on my head.

4. Nor

4. Nor hath the King of Grace decreed
    This Prize for me alone;
But all that love, and long to see
    Th' Appearance of his Son.

5. Jesus, the LORD, shall guard me safe
    From ev'ry ill Design;
And to his heav'nly Kingdom take
    This feeble Soul of mine.

6. God is my everlasting Aid,
    And Hell shall rage in vain;
To Him be highest Glory paid,
    And endless Praise. *Amen.*

HYMN LXII.

GOD's *tender Care of his Church.*

1. NOW shall my inward Joys arise,
       And burst into a Song;
   Almighty Love inspires my Heart,
       And Pleasure tunes my Tongue.

2. GOD on his thirsty Sion-Hill
       Some Mercy-Drops has thrown,
   And solemn Oaths have bound his Love
       To show'r Salvation down.

3. Why do we then indulge our Fears,
       Suspicions and Complaints?
   Is he a GOD, and shall his Grace
       Grow weary of his Saints?

4 Can a kind Woman e'er forget
    The Infant of her Womb;
And 'mongst a thousand tender Thoughts
    Her Suckling have no room?

5 "Yet, saith the Lord, should Nature change
  " And Mothers Monsters prove,
  " Sion still dwells upon the Heart
  " Of everlasting Love.

6 " Deep on the Palms of both my Hands
  " I have engrav'd her Name;
  " My Hands shall raise her ruin'd Walls,
  " And build her broken Frame."

HYMN LXIII.

Christ Jesus the Lamb of God, worshipped by all the Creation.

1 COME let us join our chearful Songs
      With Angels round the Throne;
  Ten thousand thousand are their Tongues,
      But all their Joys are one.

2 Worthy the Lamb that dy'd," they cry,
  " To be exalted thus:"
  " Worthy the Lamb," our Lips reply,
  For he was slain for us.

3 Jesus is worthy to receive
    Honour and Pow'r Divine;

And

And Blessings more than we can give,
   Be, LORD, for ever thine.

Let all that dwell above the Sky,
   And Air, and Earth, and Seas,
Conspire to lift thy Glories high,
   And speak thine endless Praise:

The whole Creation join in one,
   To bless the sacred Name
Of Him that sits upon the Throne,
   And to adore the Lamb.

HYMN LXIV.

CHRIST's *Humiliation and Exaltation.*

WHAT equal Honours shall we bring
   To thee O LORD our GOD, the Lamb,
When all the Notes that Angels sing
Are far inferior to thy Name?

Worthy is He that once was slain,
The Prince of Peace that gron'd and dy'd,
Worthy to rise, and live, and reign
At his Almighty Father's Side.

Pow'r and Dominion are his Due,
Who stood condemn'd at Pilate's Bar,
Wisdom belongs to Jesus too,
Tho' he was charg'd with Madness here.

4 All Riches are his native Right,
   Yet he sustain'd amazing Loss;
   To him ascribe eternal Might,
   Who left his Weakness on the Cross:

5 Honour immortal must be paid,
   Instead of Scandal and of Scorn:
   While Glory shines around his Head,
   And a bright Crown without a Thorn.

6 Blessings for ever on the Lamb,
   Who bore the Curse for wretched Men:
   Let Angels sound his sacred Name'
   And ev'ry Creature say, *Amen.*

HYMN LXV.

A Morning Hymn.

1 GOD of the Morning, at whose Voice
   The chearful Sun makes haste to rise,
   And like a Giant doth rejoice
   To run his Journey thro' the Skies;

2 From the fair Chambers of the East
   The Circuit of his Race begins,
   And without Weariness or Rest,
   Round the whole Earth he flies and shines:

3 Oh, like the Sun, may I fulfil
   Th' appointed Duties of the Day,

With ready Mind and active Will
March on and keep my heav'nly Way.

[4 But I shall rove and lose the Race,
If GOD, my Sun, should disappear,
And leave me in this World's wild Maze,
To follow ev'ry wand'ring Star.]

5 LORD, thy Commands are clean and pure,
Enlightning our beclouded Eyes;
Thy Threat'nings just, thy Promise sure:
Thy Gospel makes the Simple wise.

6 Give me thy Counsel for my Guide,
And then receive me to thy Bliss;
All my Desires and Hopes beside
Are faint and cold compar'd with this.

HYMN LXVI.

An Evening Hymn.

1 THUS far the LORD has led me on,
   Thus far his Pow'r prolongs my Days;
And ev'ry Ev'ning shall make known
Some fresh Memorial of his Grace.

2 Much of my Time has run to waste,
And I perhaps am near my Home;
But he forgives my Follies past,
He gives me Strength for Days to come.

3 I lay my Body down to sleep;
  Peace is the Pillow for my Head;
  While well-appointed Angels keep
  Their watchful Stations round my Bed.

4 In vain the Sons of Earth or Hell
  Tell me a thousand frightful Things;
  My GOD in safety makes me dwell
  Beneath the Shadow of his Wings.

5 Faith in his Name forbids my Fear:
  O may thy Presence ne'er depart!
  And in the Morning make me hear
  The Love and Kindness of thy Heart.

6 Thus when the Night of Death shall come,
  My Flesh shall rest beneath the Ground,
  And wait thy Voice to rouse my Tomb,
  With sweet Salvation in the Sound.]

HYMN LXVII.

Salvation, Righteousness, and Strength in CHRIST.

1 JEHOVAH speaks, let Isr'el hear,
   Let all the Earth rejoice and fear,
  While GOD's eternal Son proclaims
  His Sov'reign Honours and his Names:

2 "I am the Last, and I the First,
  "The SAVIOUR-GOD, and GOD the Just;
                "There's

"There's none besides pretends to shew
"Such Justice and Salvation too.

3 "Ye that in Shades of Darkness dwell,
"Just on the Verge of Death and Hell,
"Look up to me from distant Lands,
"Light, Life and Heav'n, are in my Hands.

"I by my holy Name have sworn,
"Nor shall the word in vain return,
"To me shall all Things bend the Knee,
"And ev'ry Tongue shall swear to me.]

"In me alone shall Men confess
"Lies all their Strength and Righteousness:
"But such as dare despise my Name,
"I'll clothe them with eternal Shame.

"In me the LORD, shall all the Seed
"Of Isr'el from their Sins be freed,
"And by their shining Graces prove
"Their Int'rest in my pard'ning Love."

HYMN LXVIII.

GOD *Holy, Just, and Sovereign.*

HOW should the Sons of Adam's Race
    Be pure before their GOD!
If he contend in Righteousness,
    We fall beneath his Rod.

2 To vindicate my Words and thoughts
    I'll make no more Pretence;
  Not one of all my thousand Faults
    Can bear a just Defence.

3 Strong is his Arm, his Heart is wise;
    What vain Presumers dare
  Against their Maker's Hand to rise
    Or tempt th' unequal War?

[4 Mountains by his Almighty Wrath
    From their old Seats are torn;
  He shakes the Earth, from South to North,
    And all her Pillars mourn.

5 He bids the Sun forbear to rise;
    Th' obedient Sun forbears:
  His Hand with Sackcloth spreads the Skies,
    And seals up all the Stars.

6 He walks upon the stormy Sea;
    Flies on the stormy Wind;
  There's none can trace his wond'rous Way,
    Or his dark Footsteps find.]

HYMN LXIX.
Joys in Heaven for a repenting Sinner.

1 WHO can describe the Joys that rise
    Thro' all the Courts of Paradise,
  To see a Prodigal return,
  To see an Heir of Glory born,

2 With Joy the Father doth approve
The Fruit of his eternal Love;
The Son with Joy looks down and sees
The Purchase of his Agonies.

3 The Spirit takes Delight to view
The holy Soul he form'd anew!
And Saints and Angels join to sing
The growing Empire of their King.

H Y M N LXX.

The Beatitudes.

[1 Bless'd are the humble Souls that see
Their Emptiness and Poverty:
Treasures of Grace to them are giv'n,
And Crowns of Joy laid up in Heav'n.]

[2 Bless'd are the Men of broken Heart,
Who mourn for Sin with inward Smart;
The Blood of CHRIST divinely flows,
A healing Balm for all their Woes.]

[3 Bless'd are the Meek, who stand afar
From Rage and Passion, Noise and War;
GOD will secure their happy State,
And plead their Cause against the Great.]

[4 Bless'd are the Souls that thirst for Grace,
Hunger and long for Righteousness;
They shall be well supply'd and fed,
With living Streams and living Bread.]

[5 Bless'd

[5 Bless'd are the Men whose Bowels move,
And melt with Sympathy and Love;
From CHRIST the LORD shall they obtain
Like Sympathy and Love again.]

[6 Bless'd are the Pure, whose Hearts are clean
From the defiling Pow'r of Sin;
With endless Pleasure they shall see
A GOD of spotless Purity.]

[7 Bless'd are the Men of peaceful Life,
Who quench the Coals of growing Strife;
They shall be call'd the Heirs of Bliss,
The Sons of GOD, the GOD of Peace.]

[8 Bless'd are the Suff'rers, who partake
Of Pain and Shame for Jesus' sake;
Their Souls shall triumph in the LORD,
Glory and Joy are their Reward.]

HYMN LXXI.

Death and immediate Glory.

1 THere is a House not made with Hands
   Eternal, and on High,
And here my Spirit waiting stands,
   'Till GOD shall bid it fly.

2 Shortly this Prison of my Clay
   Must be dissolv'd and fall;
Then, O my Soul, with Joy obey
   Thy heav'nly Father's Call.

3 'Tis

3 'Tis he, by his Almighty Grace,
   That forms thee fit for Heav'n;
And as an Earnest of the Place,
   Has his own Spirit giv'n.

4 We walk by faith of Joys to come;
   Faith lives upon his Word;
But while the Body is our Home,
   We're absent from the LORD.

5 'Tis pleasant to believe thy Grace,
   But we had rather see;
We would be absent from the Flesh,
   And present, LORD, with thee.

HYMN LXXII.

The Brazen Serpent: or, Looking to Jesus.

1 SO did the Hebrew Prophet raise
   The brazen Serpent high;
The wounded felt immediate Ease,
   The Camp forbore to die.

2 "Look upward in the dying Hour,
  "And live," the Prophet cries,
But CHRIST performs a nobler Cure,
   When Faith lifts up her eyes.

3 High on the Cross the Saviour hung,
   High in the Heav'ns he reigns;
Here Sinners, by th' old Serpent stung,
   Look and forget their Pains.

4 When

4 When God's own Son is lifted up
    A dying World revives;
The Jew beholds the glorious Hope,
    Th' expiring Gentile lives.

HYMN LXXIII.

Believers buried with Christ *in Baptism.*

1 DO we not know that solemn Word,
    That we are bury'd with the Lord;
Baptiz'd into his Death, and then
Put off the Body of our Sin?

2 Our Souls receive diviner Breath,
Rais'd from Corruption, Guilt, and Death:
So from the Grave did Christ arise,
And lives to God above the Skies.

3 No more let Sin or Satan reign
Over our mortal Flesh again:
The various Lusts we serv'd before,
Shall have Dominion now no more.

HYMN LXXIV.

The repenting Prodigal.

1 BEhold the Wretch whose Lust and Wine
    Had wasted his Estate,
He begs a Share amongst the Swine,
    To taste the Husks they eat!

2 I die

2 " I die with Hunger here he cries ;
   " I starve in foreign Lands ;
   " My Father's House has large Supplies,
   " And bounteous are his Hands.

3 " I'll go, and with a mournful Tongue
   " Fall down before his Face ;
   " Father, I've done thy Justice wrong,
   " Nor can deserve thy Grace."

4 He said, and hasten'd to his Home,
     To seek his Father's Love ;
  The Father saw the Rebel come,
     And all his Bowels move.

5 He ran, and fell upon his Neck,
     Embrac'd and kifs'd his Son :
  The Rebel's Heart with Sorrow brake,
     For Follies he had done.

6 " Take off his Clothes of Shame and Sin,"
     (The Father gives Command)
  " Dress him in Garments white and clean,
     " With Rings adorn his Hand.

7 " A Day of feasting I ordain ;
     " Let Mirth and Joy abound ;
  " My Son was dead, and lives again,
     " Was lost, and now is found."

HYMN
I

HYMN LXXV.

CHRIST's *Compassion to the Weak and Tempted.*

1 WITH Joy we meditate the Grace
    Of our High Priest above;
His Heart is made of Tenderness,
    His Bowels melt with Love.

2 Touch'd with a Sympathy within,
    He knows our feeble Frame;
He knows what sore Temptations mean,
    For he has felt the same.

3 But spotless, innocent and pure,
    The great Redeemer stood,
While Satan's fiery Darts he bore,
    And did resist to Blood.

4 He in the Days of feeble Flesh
    Pour'd out his Cries and Tears,
And in his Measure feels afresh
    What ev'ry Member bears.

[5. He'll never quench the smoking Flax,
    But raise it to a Flame;
The bruised Reed he never breaks,
    Nor scorns the meanest Name.]

6 Then let our humble Faith address
    His Mercy and his Pow'r,

We shall obtain deliv'ring Grace
In the distressing Hour.

HYMN LXXVI.

Charity and Uncharitableness.

1 NOT diff'rent Food nor diff'rent Dress,
   Compose the Kingdom of our LORD;
But Peace and Joy and Righteousness,
Faith, and Obedience to his Word.

2 When weaker Christians we despise
We do the Gospel mighty Wrong:
For GOD the Gracious and the Wise,
Receives the Feeble with the Strong.

3 Let Pride and Wrath be banish'd hence,
Meekness and Love our Souls pursue;
Nor shall our Practice give Offence
To Saints, the Gentile or the Jew.

HYMN LXXVII.

The Apostles Commission.

1 " GO preach my Gospel, saith the LORD,
   " Bid the whole Earth my Grace
    ' receive:
" He shall be sav'd that trusts my Word;
" He shall be damn'd that won't believe.

[2 " I'll

[2 " I'll make your great Commiffion known,.
" And ye fhall prove my Gofpel true,
" By all the Works that I have done,
" By all the Wonders ye fhall do.

3 " Go heal the Sick, go raife the Dead,
" Go caft out Devils in my Name;
" Nor let my Prophets be afraid, (pheme.]
" Tho' Greeks reproach, and Jews blaf-.

4 " Teach all the Nations my Commands;
" I'm with you till the World fhall end;
" All Pow'r is trufted in my Hands,
" I can deftroy, and can defend."

5 He fpake, and Light fhone round his Head;
On a bright Cloud to Heav'n he rode:
They to the fartheft Nations fpread
The Grace of their afcended GOD.

HYMN LXXVIII.
Love and Hatred.

1 NOW by the Bowels of my GOD,
His fharp Diftrefs, his fore Complaints,.
By his laft Groans, his dying Blood,
I charge my Soul to love the Saints.

2 Clamour and Wrath and War be gone,
Envy and Spite for ever ceafe;
Let bitter Words no more be known
Amongft the Saints, the Sons of Peace.

3 The

3 The Spirit, like a peaceful Dove,
Flies from the Realms of Noise and Strife;
Why should we vex and grieve his Love,
Who seals our Souls to heav'nly Life?

4 Tender and kind be all our Thoughts;
Thro' all our Lives let Mercy run:
So GOD forgives our num'rous Faults,
For the dear Sake of CHRIST his Son.

HYMN LXXIX.

Holiness and Grace.

1 SO let our Lips and Lives express
The holy Gospel we profess;
So let our Works and Virtues shine,
To prove the Doctrine all divine.

2 Thus shall we best proclaim abroad
The Honours of our SAVIOUR-GOD;
When the Salvation reigns within,
And Grace subdues the Pow'r of Sin.

3 Our Flesh and Sense must be deny'd,
Passion and Envy, Lust and Pride;
Whilst Justice, Temp'rance, Truth and Love,
Our inward Piety approve.

4 Religion bears our Spirits up,
While we expect that blessed Hope,
The bright Appearance of the LORD,
And Faith stands leaning on his Word.

HYMN LXXX.

The Love of CHRIST *shed abroad in the Heart.*

1 COme, dearest LORD, descend and dwell
 By Faith and Love in ev'ry Breast;
Then shall we know, and taste, and feel
The Joys that cannot be express'd.

2 Come, fill our Hearts with inward Strength,
Make our enlarged Souls possess,
And learn the Heighth, and Breadth, and Length,
Of thine unmeasurable Grace.

3 Now to the GOD whose Pow'r can do
More than our Thoughts and Wishes know,
Be everlasting Honours done
By all the Church, thro' CHRIST his Son.

HYMN LXXXI.

The Witnessing and Sealing Spirit.

1 WHY should the Children of a King
 Go mourning all their Days?
Great Comforter! descend and bring
Some Tokens of thy Grace.

2 Dost thou not dwell in all the Saints,
And seal the Heirs of Heav'n?
When wilt thou banish my Complaints,
And shew my Sins forgiv'n?

3 Assure my Conscience of her Part
In the Redeemer's Blood;
And bear thy Witness with my Heart,
That I am born of GOD.

4 Thou art the Earnest of his Love,
  The Pledge of Joys to come;
And thy soft Wings, celestial Dove,
  Will safe convey me home.

HYMN LXXXII.

CHRIST and Aaron, taken from Heb. vii *and* ix.

JESUS, in thee our Eyes behold
  A thousand Glories more
Than the rich Gems and polish'd Gold
  The Sons of Aaron wore.

They first their own Burnt-off'rings brought,
  To purge themselves from Sin;
Thy Life was pure without a Spot,
  And all thy Nature clean.

3 Fresh Blood, as constant as the Day,
  Was on their Altar spilt;
But thy one Off'ring takes away
  For ever all our Guilt.]

4 Their Priesthood ran thro' sev'ral Hands,
  For mortal was their Race:
Thy never-changing Office stands,
  Eternal as thy Days.]

5 Once in the Circuit of a Year,
  With Blood, but not his own,
Aaron within the Veil appears,
  Before the golden Throne.

6 But CHRIST by his own pow'rful Blood
  Ascends above the Skies,

And

And in the Prefence of our GOD
Shews his own Sacrifice.]

7 JESUS, the King of Glory, reigns
On Sion's heav'nly Hill;
Looks like a Lamb that has been flain,
And wears his Priefthood ftill.

8 He ever lives to intercede
Before his Father's Face:
Give him, my Soul, thy Caufe to plead,
Nor doubt the Father's Grace.

HYMN LXXXIII.
Characters of CHRIST.

1 GO worfhip at IMMANUEL's Feet,
See in his Face what Wonders meet!
Earth is too narrow to exprefs
His Worth, his Glory, or his Grace.

[2 The whole Creation can afford
But fome faint Shadows of my LORD;
Nature, to make his Beauties known,
Muft mingle Colours not her own.]

[3 Is he compar'd to Wine or Bread?
Dear LORD! our Souls would thus be fed:
That Flefh, that dying Blood of thine,
Is Bread of Life, is heav'nly Wine.]

[4 Is he a Tree? The World receives
Salvation from his healing Leaves:
That righteous Branch, that fruitful Bough,
Is David's Root and Offspring too.]

[5 Is he a Rose? Not Sharon yields
Such Fragrancy in all her Fields:
Or if the Lilly he assume,
The Vallies bless the rich Perfume.]

[6 Is he a Vine? his heav'nly Root
Supplies the Boughs with Life and Fruit.
O let a lasting Union join
My Soul to Christ the living Vine!]

[7 Is he a Head? Each Member lives,
And owns the vital Pow'r he gives;
The Saints below and Saints above,
Join'd by his Spirit and his Love.]

[8 Is he a Fountain? There I bathe,
And heal the Plague of Sin and Death:
These Waters all my Soul renew,
And cleanse my spotted Garments too.]

[9 Is he a Fire? He'll purge my Dross:
But the true Gold sustains no Loss:
Like a Refiner shall he sit,
And tread the Refuse with his Feet.]

[10 Is he a Rock? How firm he proves!
The Rock of Ages never moves;
Yet the sweet Streams that from him flow
Attend us all the Desart thro'.]

[11 Is he a Way? He leads to God,
The Path is drawn in Lines of Blood;
There would I walk with Hope and Zeal,
'Till I arrive at Sion's Hill.]

[12 Is he a Door? I'll enter in;
Behold the Pastures large and green;

    A Paradise divinely fair,
  None but the Sheep have Freedom there.]

[13 Is he design'd the Corner-Stone,
    For Men to build their Heav'n upon?
    I'll make him my Foundation too,
  Nor fear the Plots of Hell below.]

[14 Is he a Temple? I adore
    Th' indwelling Majesty and Pow'r;
    And still to his most holy Place,
  Whene'er I pray, I'll turn my Face.]

[15 Is he a Star? He breaks the Night,
    Piercing the Shades with dawning Light;
    I know his Glories from afar,
  I know the bright, the Morning-Star.]

[16 Is he a Sun? His Beams are Grace,
    His Course is Joy and Righteousness:
    Nations rejoice when he appears
  To chase their Clouds, and dry their Tears.

17 O let me climb those higher Skies,
    Where Storms and Darkness never rise!
    There he displays his Pow'rs abroad,
  And shines and reigns th' Incarnate GOD.]

18 Nor Earth, nor Seas, nor Sun, nor Stars,
    Nor Heav'n his full Resemblance bears;
    His Beauties we can never trace,
  Till we behold him Face to Face.

HYMN LXXXIV.

The same as the cxlviiith *Psalm.*

1 JOIN all the glorious Names
   Of Wisdom, Love and Pow'r,
That ever Mortals knew,
That Angels ever bore:
    All are too mean
    To speak his Worth,
    Too mean to set
    My SAVIOUR forth.

2 But, O what gentle Terms,
What condescending Ways
Doth our REDEEMER use
To teach his heav'nly Grace!
    Mine Eyes with Joy
    And Wonder see
    What Forms of Love
    He bears for me.

[3 Array'd in mortal Flesh,
He like an ANGEL stands,
And holds the Promises
And Pardons in his Hands:
    Commission'd from
    His Father's Throne,
    To make his Grace
    To Mortals known.]

[4 Great PROPHET of my GOD,
My Tongue would bless thy Name;
By thee the joyful News
Of our Salvation came:

The joyful News
Of Sins forgiv'n,
Of Hell fubdu'd,
And Peace with Heav'n.]

[5 Be thou my COUNSELLOR,
My PATTERN, and my GUIDE;
And thro' this defart Land
Still keep me near thy Side.
   O let my Feet
   Ne'er run aftray,
   Nor rove, nor feek
   The crooked Way!]

[6 I love my SHEPHERD's Voice,
His watchful Eyes fhall keep
My wand'ring Soul among
The Thoufands of his Sheep:
   He feeds his Flock,
   He calls their Names,
   His Bofom bears
   The tender Lambs.]

[7 To this dear SURETY's Hand
Will I commit my Caufe;
He anfwers and fulfils
His Father's broken Laws.
   Behold my Soul
   At Freedom fet;
   My Surety paid
   The dreadful Debt.

[8 JESUS, my great HIGH PRIEST,
Offer'd his Blood and dy'd;
My guilty Confcience feeks
No Sacrifice befide.

His

His pow'rful Blood
Did once atone;
And now it pleads
Before the Throne.]

9 My ADVOCATE appears
For my Defence on high;
The Father bows his Ears,
And lays his Thunder by.
　　Not all that Hell
　　Or Sin can say,
　　Shall turn his Heart,
　　His Love away.]

[10 My dear Almighty LORD,
My CONQU'ROR and my KING,
Thy Scepter, and thy Sword,
Thy reigning Grace I sing.
　　Thine is the Pow'r;
　　Behold I sit
　　In willing Bonds
　　Beneath thy Feet.

[11 Now let my Soul arise,
And tread the Tempter down:
My CAPTAIN leads me forth
To Conquest and a Crown.
　　A feeble Saint
　　Shall win the Day,
　　Tho' Death and Hell
　　Obstruct the Way.]

12 Should all the Hosts of Death,
   And Pow'rs of Hell unknown,
   Put their most dreadful Forms
   Of Rage and Mischief on,
     I shall be safe;
     For Christ displays
     Superior Pow'r
     And guardian Grace.

HYMN LXXXV.

1 LET ev'ry mortal ear attend,
     And ev'ry heart rejoice,
   The trumpet of the gospel sounds,
     With an inviting voice.

2 Come all ye hungry starving souls,
     That feed upon the wind,
   And vainly strive, with earthly toys,
     To fill an empty mind.

3 Eternal wisdom has prepar'd
     A soul-reviving feast;
   And bids your longing appetites
     The rich provision taste.

4 Ho! ye that pant for living streams,
     And pine away and die;
   Here you may quench your raging thirst
     With springs that never dry.

5 Rivers of love and mercy here
     In a rich ocean join;

Salvation in abundance flows,
    Like floods of milk and wine.

6 Dear God! the treasures of thy love
    Are everlasting mines;
  Deep as our helpless mis'ries are,
    And boundless as our sins.

7 The happy gates of gospel grace
    Stand open night and day;
  Lord, we are come to seek supplies,
    And drive our wants away.

HYMN LXXXVI.

1 NOW may the Spirit's holy fire,
    Descending from above,
  His waiting family inspire
    With joy, and peace, and love!

2 Thee we the Comforter confess;
    Unless thou'rt present here;
  Our songs of praise are vain address,
    We utter heartless pray'r.

3 Wake heav'nly wind, arise and come,
    Blow on the drooping field;
  Our spices then shall breathe perfume,
    And fragrant incense yield.

4 Touch, with a living coal, the lip
    That shall proclaim thy word;

And bid each awful hearer keep
  Attention to the Lord.

5 Hasten the restitution-day,
  Which now corruption shrouds;
New heavens, and new earth display,
  With Jesus in the clouds.

HYMN LXXXVII.

1 LORD, we come before thee now,
    At thy feet we humbly bow:
  Oh! do not our suit disdain,
  Shall we seek thee, Lord, in vain?

2 Lord, on thee our souls depend,
  In compassion now descend:
  Fill our hearts with thy rich grace,
  Tune our lips to sing thy praise.

3 In thine own appointed way,
  Now we seek thee, here we stay;
  Lord we know not how to go
  'Till a blessing thou bestow.

4 Send some message from thy word,
  That may joy and peace afford;
  Let thy Spirit now impart
  Full salvation to each heart.

5 Comfort those who weep and mourn,
  Let the time of joy return;

Those that are cast down, lift up,
Make them strong in faith and hope!

6 Grant that all may seek and find
Thee a gracious God and kind;
Heal the sick, the captive free,
Let us all rejoice in thee!

HYMN LXXXVIII.

1 FATHER, I stretch my hands to thee,
    No other help I know;
If thou withdraw thyself from me,
    Ah! whither shall I go?

2 What did thine only Son endure,
    Before I drew my breath?
What pain, what labour to secure
    My soul from endless death!

3 O Jesu, could I this believe,
    I now should feel thy pow'r;
Now my poor soul thou would'st retrieve,
    Nor let me wait one hour.

4 Author of faith, to thee I lift
    My weary, longing eyes;
O let me now receive that gift!
    My soul without it dies!

HYMN LXXXIX.

1 LIGHT of those whose dreary dwelling
    Borders on the shades of death,
Come! and by thy love's revealing,
    Dissipate the clouds beneath:
The new heav'n and earth's creator,
    In our deepest darkness rise!
Scatt'ring all the night of nature,
    Pouring eye-sight on our eyes!

2 Still we wait for thine appearing
    Life and joy thy beams impart;
Chasing all our fears, and chearing
    Ev'ry poor benighted heart:
Come, and manifest the favour
    God hath for our ransom'd race;
Come, thou universal Saviour,
    Come, and bring thy gospel-grace.

3 Save us in thy great compassion,
    O thou mild pacific prince!
Give the knowledge of salvation,
    Give the pardon of our sins!
By thine all-restoring merit,
    Ev'ry burthen'd soul release,
Ev'ry weary, wand'ring spirit
    Guide into thy perfect peace.

HYMN XC.

1 O Lord! to whom for help I call,
    Thy miracles repeat;

With pitying eye behold me fall
  A leper at thy feet.

2 Loathsome, and foul, and self abhorr'd,
  I sink beneath my sin;
  But, if thou wilt, a gracious word
  Of thine can make me clean.

3 Thou seest me deaf to thy commands,
  Open O Lord! mine ear;
  Bid me stretch out my wither'd hands,
  And lift them up in pray'r.

4 Silent (alas! thou know'st how long!)
  My voice I cannot raise;
  But, O! when thou shalt loose my tongue,
  The dumb shall sing thy praise.

5 Lame at the pool I still am found;
  Give, and my strength employ;
  Light as an hart I then shall bound,
  The lame shall leap for joy.

6 Blind from my birth to guilt and thee,
  And dark I am within;
  The love of God I cannot see,
  Nor sinfulness of sin.

7 But thou, they say, art passing by,
  O let me find thee near!
  Jesus, in mercy hear my cry,
  Thou son of David, hear!

8 Long

8 Long have I waited in the way,
   For thee, the heav'nly light;
Command me to be brought, and say,
   " Sinner, receive thy sight."

HYMN XCI.

1 JESU, Redeemer, Saviour, Lord,
   The weary sinner's friend:
Come to my help, pronounce the word,
   Bid my corruptions end.

2 Thou canst o'ercome this heart of mine,
   Thou canst victorious prove;
For everlasting strength is thine,
   And everlasting love.

3 Thy pow'rful Spirit can subdue
   Unconquerable sin;
Cleanse my foul heart, and make it new,
   And write thy law within.

4 Bound down with twice ten thousand ties,
   Yet let me hear thy call;
My soul in confidence shall rise,
   Shall rise and break thro' all.

5 Speak, and the deaf shall hear thy voice,
   The blind his sight receive,
The dumb in songs of praise rejoice,
   The heart of stone believe.

6 The Æthiop then shall change his skin,
　　The dead shall feel thy pow'r;
　The loathsome leper shall be clean,
　　And I shall sin abhor.

HYMN XCII.

1 O for an heart to love my God!—
　　An heart from sin set free;
　An heart that always feels the blood,
　　So freely shed for me!

2 An heart resign'd, submissive, meek,
　　My dear Redeemer's throne;
　Where only Christ is heard to speak,
　　Where Jesus reigns alone.

3 An humble, lowly, contrite heart,—
　　Believing, true and clean;
　Which neither life nor death can part
　　From him that dwells within.

4 An heart in ev'ry thought renew'd,
　　And fill'd with love divine:
　Perfect and right, and pure, and good,
　　A copy, Lord! of thine.

5 Thy tender heart is still the same,
　　And melts at human woe;
　Send down thy grace, O blessed Lamb!
　　That I thy love may know.

6 Thy holy nature Lord! impart
　　Come quickly from above;
　Write thy new name upon my heart,
　　Thy new best name of Love.

HYMN XCIII.

1 O Thou, whose tender mercy hears
　　Contrition's humble sigh;
　Whose hand, indulgent, wipes the tears
　　From sorrow's weeping eye.

2 See! low before the throne of grace
　　A wretched wand'rer mourn;
　Hast thou not bid me seek thy face?
　　Hast thou not said, Return?

3 And shall my guilty fears prevail
　　To drive me from thy feet?
　O let not this dear refuge fail,
　　This only safe retreat.

4 Absent from thee, my guide, my light,
　　Without one chearing ray,
　Thro' dangers, fears, and gloomy night,
　　How desolate my way!

5 O shine on this benighted heart,
　　With beams of mercy shine;
　And let thy healing voice impart
　　A taste of joys divine.

　　　　　　　　　　　　Thy

Thy presence only can bestow
  Delights which never cloy;
Be this my solace, here below,
  And my eternal joy.

HYMN XCIV.

ON thee, O God of purity,
  I wait for hallowing grace;
None without holiness shall see
  The glories of thy face:
In souls unholy, and unclean,
  Thou never canst delight;
Nor shall they, while unsav'd from sin,
  Appear before thy sight.

But as for me, with humble fear,
  I will approach thy gate;
Though most unworthy to draw near,
  Or in thy courts to wait:
I trust in thine unbounded grace,
  To all so freely giv'n;
And worship t'ward thy holy place,
  And lift my soul to heav'n.

Lead me in all thy righteous ways,
  Nor suffer me to slide;
Point out the path before my face,
  My God be thou my guide!
O may I ne'er to evil yield,
  Defended from above,
And kept, and cover'd with the shield
  Of thine Almighty love.

HYMN

HYMN XCV.

1 THE one thing needful, that good part,
  Which Mary chose with all her heart,
  I would pursue with heart and mind,
  And seek unweary'd till I find.

2 But, oh! I'm blind and ignorant,
  The Spirit of the Lord I want;
  To guide me in the narrow road,
  That leads to happiness and God.

3 O Lord, my God, to thee I pray,
  Teach me to know, and find the way
  How I may have my sins forgiv'n,
  And safe, and surely get to heav'n.

4 My mind enlighten with thy light,
  That I may understand aright
  The glorious gospel-mystery,
  Which shews the way to heav'n and thee.

5 Hidden in Christ the treasure lies,
  That goodly pearl of so great price;
  No other way but Christ, there is
  To endless happiness and bliss.

6 O Jesus Christ, my Lord and God,
  Who hast redeem'd me by thy blood;
  Unite my heart so fast to thee,
  That we may never parted be.

HYMN XCVI.

A Sinner's Prayer.

1 O My Lord, what muſt I do?
　Only thou the way canſt ſhew;
Thou canſt ſave me in this hour,
I have neither will nor pow'r:
God if over all thou art,
Greater than the ſinful heart;
Let it now on me be ſhown,
Take away the heart of ſtone.

2 Take away my darling ſin,
Make me willing to be clean;
Make me willing to receive
What thy goodneſs waits to give:
Force me, Lord, with all to part,
Tear all idols from my heart;
Let thy pow'r on me be ſhown,
Take away the heart of ſtone.

3 Jeſu, mighty to renew,
Work in me, to will and do;
Turn my nature's rapid tide,
Stem the torrent of my pride,
Stop the whirlwind of my will,
Bid corruptions, Lord, be ſtill;
Now thy love almighty ſhew,
Make e'en me a creature new.

4 Arm of God, thy strength put on,
Bow the heavens, and come down;
All mine unbelief o'erthrow,
Lay th' aspiring mountain low;
Conquer thy worst foe in me,
Get thyself the victory,
Save the vilest of the race,
Force me to be sav'd by grace.

HYMN XCVII.

To Jesus Christ.

1 COME, let us all unite to praise
    The Saviour of mankind,
Our thankful hearts in solemn lays,
    Be with our voices join'd.

2 But how shall dust his worth declare,
    When angels try in vain;
Their faces veil when they appear
    Before the son of man.

3 O Lord, we cannot silent be,
    By love we are constrain'd
To offer our best thanks to thee,——
    Our Saviour, and our friend!

4 Tho' feeble are our best essays,
    Thy love will not despise;
Our grateful songs of humble praise,
    Our well-meant sacrifice.

5 Let ev'ry tongue thy goodnefs fhow,
    And fpread abroad thy fame;
Let ev'ry heart with praife o'erflow,
    And blefs thy facred name!

6 Worfhip and honour, thanks and love,
    Be to our Jefus giv'n!
By men below,---by hofts above---
    By all in earth and heav'n!

HYMN XCVIII.

Redeeming Love.

1 NOW begin the heav'nly theme,
    Sing aloud in Jefu's name;
Ye, who Jefu's kindnefs prove,
Triumph in redeeming love.

2 Ye, who fee the Father's grace,
Beaming in the Saviour's face;
As to Canaan on ye move,
Praife and blefs redeeming love.

3 Mourning fouls dry up your tears,
Banifh all your guilty fears;
See your guilt and curfe remove,
Cancell'd by redeeming love.

4 Ye, alas! who long have been
Willing flaves of death and fin;
Now from blifs no longer rove,
Stop---and tafte redeeming love.

                    5 Welcome

5 Welcome all by sin opprest,
Welcome all to Jesus Christ;
Nothing brought him from above,
Nothing but redeeming love.

6 He subdu'd th' infernal pow'rs,
His tremendous foes and ours,
From their cursed empire drove,
Mighty in redeeming love.

7 Hither then your music bring,
Strike aloud each joyful string;
Mortals join the hosts above,
Join to praise redeeming love.

HYMN XCIX.

1 YE servants of God,
    Your master proclaim;
And publish abroad
    His wonderful name:
The name all-victorious
    Of Jesus extol;
His kingdom is glorious,
    And rules over all.

2   God ruleth on high,
    Almighty to save;
And still he is nigh,
    His presence we have:
The great congregation
    His triumph shall sing,

Ascribing

Ascribing salvation
  To Jesus our king.

3 Salvation to God,
  Who sits on the throne;
Let all cry aloud,
  And honour the son:
Our Jesus's praises
  The angels proclaim,
Fall down on their faces,
  And worship the Lamb.

4 Then let us adore,
  And give him his right;
All glory and pow'r,
  And wisdom and might;
All honour and blessing,
  With angels above;
And thanks never ceasing,
  And infinite love.

HYMN C.

Te Deum.

1. HOW can we adore,
    Or worthily praise,
Thy goodness and pow'r,
  Thou God of all grace!
With honour and blessing
  Before thee we fall,
Most gladly confessing
  Thee Father of all.

2 The heavens and earth,
     And water and air,
  To thee owe their birth,
     Subsist by thy care;
  While angels are singing
     Thy praises above,
  We mortals are bringing
     Our tribute of love.

3 Thou Saviour, art one
     With God the supreme;
  His eternal son,
     And equal with him:
  Invested with glory,
     On high dost thou sit,
  While angels adore thee,
     And bow at thy feet.

4 How great was thy love!
     How wondrous thy grace!
  Thou cam'st from above,
     To save a lost race;
  And man to deliver,
     Of woman was born,
  That ev'ry believer
     To God might return.

5 How soon will thy seat
     Of judgment appear!
  Prepare us to meet,
     And welcome thee there!
  Thy witnessing Spirit

In us shed abroad;
And bid us inherit
The kingdom of God!

HYMN CI.

Christ our Righteousness.

1 JESU, thy blood and righteousness,
   My beauty are, my glorious dress;
'Midst flaming worlds in these array'd,
With joy shall I lift up my head.

2 When from the dust of death I rise,
To claim my mansion in the skies;
E'en then shall this be all my plea,
" Jesus hath LIV'D, hath DY'D for me."

3 Bold shall I stand in that great day,
For who ought to my charge shall lay?
Fully thro' these absolv'd I am
From sin and fear, from guilt and shame.

4 Thus Abraham, the friend of God,
Thus all the armies bought with blood,
Saviour of sinners thee proclaim;
Sinners, of whom the chief I am.

5 This spotless robe the same appears,
When ruin'd nature sinks in years;
No age can change its glorious hue,
The grace of Christ is ever new.

6 O Jesu Christ, all praise to Thee,
That thou a man vouchsaf'd to be;
And for each Soul, which thou hast made,
Hast an eternal Ransom paid.

7 I do believe if sinners Race
Ten thousand times more num'rous was;
Yet still the Devil had his full,
'Tis without right he keeps one soul.

8 Ah, give to all thy servants, Lord,
With pow'r to speak thy quick'ning word,
That all who to thy wounds will flee,
May find eternal life in Thee.

9 Thou God of might, thou God of love,
Let all the world thy mercy prove;
Now let thy word o'er all prevail,
Now take the spoils of death and hell.

10 O let the dead now hear thy voice;
Now bid thy banish'd ones rejoice;
Their beauty this, their glorious dress,
Jesus, the Lord OUR RIGHTEOUSNESS.

HYMN CII.

Striving to praise Christ.

1 LET us, the sheep by Jesus nam'd,
  Our shepherd's mercy bless;
Let us, whom Jesus hath redeem'd
  Shew forth our thankfulness.

2 Not

2 Not unto us, to thee alone,
    Be praife and glory giv'n;
Here fhall thy praifes be begun,
    But carry'd on in heav'n.

3 The hofts of fpirits now with thee,
    Eternal anthems fing;
To imitate them here, lo! we
    Our hallelujahs bring.

4 Had we our tongues like them infpir'd,
    Like theirs our fongs fhould rife;
Like them we never fhould be tir'd,
    But love the facrifice.

5 'Till we this veil of flefh lay down,
    Accept our weaker lays;
And when, O Lord, we reach thy throne,
    We'll join in nobler praife,

H Y M N CIII.

Refting under the Crofs.

1 CHildren of *Ifrael* fee what fhade,
    The crofs does us afford;
It was for weary trav'llers made,
    We thank thee for it, Lord.

2 Here let us fit, and all prepare
    To fing his worthy fame;
Who to redeem us fojourn'd here,
    Chrift Jefus is his name.

3 We sing thy suff'rings, wounds and blood,
    The virtue of thy pain:
  We sing thy griefs, thou Son of God,
    Thou Lamb for sinners slain.

4 We hail thee, thou by Jews revil'd,
    To thee we bow the knee;
  Hail! very God, the promis'd child,
    The prophets sang of thee.

5 While others praise an unknown God,
    We each will sing of thee;
  " Jesus has wash'd me in his blood,
    And liv'd, and dy'd for me."

HYMN CIV.

1 O Come, thou wounded Lamb of God;
    Come, wash us in thy cleansing blood!
  Give us to know thy love, then pain
  Is sweet, and life or death is gain.

2 Take our poor hearts, and let them be
  For ever clos'd to all but thee;
  Seal thou our breasts, and let us wear
  That pledge of love for ever there.

3 How can it be thou heav'nly king,
  That thou should man to glory bring!
  Make slaves the partners of thy throne,
  And give them an immortal crown!

4 Ah, Lord! enlarge our scanty thought;
  To know the wonders thou hast wrought;
                     Unloose

Unloose our stamm'ring tongues to tell
Thy love immense, unsearchable.

5 First-born of many brethren, thou,
To thee both earth and heav'n must bow;
Help us to thee our all to give,
Thine may we die, thine may we live!

HYMN CV.

1 DIsciples of Christ,
    Ye friends of the Lamb;
Attend, and assist
    In singing his fame:
Eternal thanksgiving
    The faithful should pay,
The living, the living,
    As we do this day.

2 A body of clay
    He humbly put on,
And then took away
    The sin we had done;
And in it endured
    The wrath to us due,
The curse we incurred,
    Our stripes and our woe.

3 Not only he dy'd,
    But also arose;
Laid weakness aside,
    And over his foes,

(Sin, death and the devil,)
   He triumph'd, and o'er
This world, and all evil,
   Dominion and pow'r.

4 O merciful Lamb,
   Who sits on the throne,
We bow at thy name,
   Thee Saviour we own,
Deserving our blessing,
   And blessing we'll give,
Without ever ceasing,
   So long as we live.

HYMN CVI.

An happy moment.

1 SAviour, I do feel thy merit,
   Sprinkled with redeeming blood;
And my weary troubled spirit
   Now finds rest in thee, my God:
I am safe, and I am happy,
   While in thy dear arms I lie;
Sin and satan cannot hurt me,
   When the Saviour is so nigh.

2 Now I'll sing of Jesu's merit,
   Tell the world of his dear name;
That if any want his Spirit,
   He is still the very same:
He that asketh, soon receiveth,
   He that seeks is sure to find;
Come, for whosoe'er believeth,
   He will never cast behind.

3 Now our advocate is pleading
    With his Father, and our God;
Now for us he's interceeding,
    As the purchafe of his blood:
Now methinks I hear him praying,
    Father, fave them, I have dy'd;
And the Father, anfwers, faying,
    They are freely juftify'd.

HYMN CVII.

Adoring Chrift.

1 O For a thoufand tongues to fing,
    My dear Redeemer's praife!
The glories of my God and king,
    The triumphs of his grace.

2 Jefus, the name that charms our fears,
    That bids our forrows ceafe;
'Tis mufic in the finner's ears,
    'Tis life, and health, and peace.

3 He breaks the pow'r of cancel'd fin,
    He fets the pris'ners free;
His blood can make the fouleft clean,
    His blood avail'd for me.

4 He fpeaks, and lift'ning to his voice,
    New life the dead receive;
The mournful, broken hearts rejoice,
    The humble poor believe.

5 Hear

5 Hear him, ye deaf; his praise, ye dumb,
Your loosen'd tongues employ;
Ye blind, behold your Saviour come,
And leap, ye lame, for joy.

HYMN CXI.

Praise to the Redeemer.

1 PLung'd in a gulph of dark despair,
We wretched sinners lay,
Without one cheering beam of hope,
Or spark of glimm'ring day.

2 With pitying eyes the prince of grace
Beheld our helpless grief;
He saw, and (O amazing love!)
He ran to our relief.

3 Down from the shining seats above,
With joyful haste he fled;
Enter'd the grave in mortal flesh,
And dwelt among the dead.

4 Oh! for this love, let rocks and hills
Their lasting silence break;
And all harmonious human tongues
The Saviour's praises speak.

5 Angels assist our mighty joys,
Strike all your harps of gold;
But when you raise your highest notes,
His love can ne'er be told.

HYMN

HYMN CXII.

Human Weakness owned.

1 MY Lord, how great's the favour!
 That I a sinner poor,
Can thro' thy blood's sweet favour
 Approach thy mercy's door:
And find an open passage
 Unto the throne of grace;
There wait the welcome message,
 That bids me go in peace.

2 Lord, I'm an helpless creature,
 Full of the deepest need,
Throughout defil'd by nature
 Stupid, and inly dead:
My strength is perfect weakness,
 And all I have is sin;
My heart is all uncleanness,
 A den of thieves within.

3 In this forlorn condition,
 Who shall afford me aid?
Where shall I find compassion
 But in the church's head?
Jesus, thou art all pity,
 O take me to thine arms,
And exercise thy mercy,
 To save me from all harms.

4 I'll

4 I'll never cease repeating
    My numberless complaints;
But ever be entreating
    The glorious king of saints,
'Till I attain the image
    Of him I inly love;
And pay my grateful homage
    With all the saints above.

5 Then I, with all in glory,
    Will thankfully relate
Th' amazing, pleasing story
    Of Jesu's love so great;
In this blest contemplation
    I ever shall be well;
And prove such consolation,
    As none below can tell.

HYMN CX.
Judgment.

PRESS'D my soul with future prospects,
    Sing creation's dismal end
Long foretold by sacred prophets,
Holy muse thy succours lend,
Say what horror what confusion!
Will each sinful heart dismay;
What distresses, tortures, anguish
Reign in that tremenduous day?

Rumbling thunders, forky lightnings
Ghastly glaring thwart the gloom;
                                Nature

Nature, shaking to her center,
Groans, prophetic of her doom.
Cliffy rocks and lofty mountains
Oe'r their trembling bases rock;
While earth yawns in dreadful chasms,
With each strong repeated shock.

Seas, with horrid palpitation,
Ravage round their frighten'd shores;
Blust'ring wind with frantic fury,
Through each ruin'd fabric roars.
The sun's bright orb is veil'd in sackloth,
Stripp'd of all his sparkling beams;
The moon has drop'd her silver radiance,
And dissolves in purple streams.

Stars, of late, divinely brilliant,
Studding Night's cimmerian robe;
Hurl'd in darkness from their orbits,
Each a darken'd, ruin'd globe.
Hark! the martial trumpet sounding,
Rends in twain the crystal sky;
Vengeance blazing lights the concave
Of profound eternity.

See the sov'reign æther furling;
Nobler scenes salute mine eyes;
Heav'n in solemn pomp descending,
Crimson banners dress the skies,
On the arched, striped rainbow
Sits enthron'd th' eternal God;
Myriads of celestial warriors
Round him wait his awful nod.

Go, he cries, ye winged heralds,
Bring my faints from ev'ry wind;
Thofe my blood from death hath ranfom'd,
Thofe in life's fair volume penn'd.
Strait a holy troop obfequious,
Swift as lightning fkimm'd along;
And from ev'ry grave collecting
Jefus's dear redeemed throng.

Death no more with livid afpect,
Spurs his fallow fteed to flay;
Now the rav'nous foe difgorges
All his long imprifon'd prey:
Rous'd from tombs each wicked rifes,
By the trumpet's thrilling found;
Round they ftare with wild amazement,
Wond'ring at the fcene profound.

Fill'd with horror, dread and anguifh,
Rocks and mountains they implore,
To fall and crufh them out of being;
Wifhing now to be no more.
Hark! the herald calls to judgment;
Juftice draws the glitt'ring fword;
Lightning glances from his afpect;
Thunders clothe his awful word.

Go ye curfed fill'd with vengeance,
Nor for peace my name invoke;
Ye who once defpis'd my mercy,
And my fury dare provoke,
Go to pits of burning Sulphur,

Ever

Ever banish'd from my rest;
Where the soul's eternal larum,
Ceaseless beats your pulsive breast.

He spoke, he spoke; and from his visage flash'd
    his ire,
And wrapp'd the earth and seas in liquid fire;
Hell groan'd, hell groan'd, and heav'n ascended
    with a song,
And the eternal ages roll,d along.
Hell groan'd hell groan'd and heav'n ascended
    with a song,
And the eternal ages roll'd along.

HYMN CXI.

Another.

1 LO! he cometh, countless trumpets
    Blow before the bloody sign;
  Midst ten thousand saints and angels,
    See the crucified shine.
        Hallelujah! hallelujah! hallelujah!
  Welcome, welcome, bleeding Lamb!

2 Now his merit, by the harpers,
    Thro' th' eternal deep resounds;
  Now resplendent shine his nail-prints,
    Ev'ry eye shall see his wounds:
        They who pierc'd him, they who
            pierc'd him, they who pierc'd him,
  Shall at his appearance wail.

3 Ev'ry

3 Ev'ry island, sea, and mountain,
　　Heav'n and earth shall flee away;
　All who hate him, must, ashamed,
　　Hear the trump proclaim the day:
　　　Come to judgment, come to judg-
　　　ment, come to judgment,
　Stand before the Son of man.

4 Saints who love him, view his glory
　　Shining in his bruised face,
　His dear person on the rainbow,
　　Now his peoples head shall raise:
　　　Happy mourners, happy mourners,
　　　happy mourners,
　Lo! in clouds he comes, he comes!

5 Now redemption, long expected,
　　See in solemn pomp appear;
　All his people once rejected,
　　Now shall meet him in the air:
　　　Hallelujah! hallelujah! hallelujah!
　Now the promis'd kingdom's come.

6 View him smiling, now determin'd
　　Ev'ry evil to destroy;
　All the nations now shall sing him
　　Songs of everlasting joy:
　　　O come quickly, O come quickly,
　　　O come quickly,
　Hallelujah! come, Lord, come.

HYMN

HYMN CXII.

God the only Refuge in Trouble.

1 DEAR Refuge of my weary foul,
   On thee when forrows rife;
On thee, when waves of trouble roll,
   My fainting hope relies.

2 While hope revives, tho' prefs'd with fears,
   And I can fay, " My God,"
Beneath thy feet I fpread my cares,
   And pour my woes abroad.

3 To thee I tell each rifing grief,
   For thou alone canft heal;
Thy word can bring a fweet relief,
   For ev'ry pain I feel.

4 But oh! when gloomy doubts prevail
   I fear to call thee mine;
The fprings of comfort feem to fail,
   And all my hopes decline.

5 Yet gracious God, where fhall I flee?
   Thou art my only truft;
And ftill my foul wou'd cleave to thee,
   Tho' proftrate in the duft.

6 Haft thou not bid me feek thy face?
   And fhall I feek in vain?

And

And can the ear of fov'reign grace
Be deaf when I complain?

7 No, ſtill the ear of fov'reign grace
Attends the mourner's prayer;
O may I ever find acceſs,
To breathe my ſorrows there.

8 Thy mercy-ſeat is open ſtill;
Here let my ſoul retreat,
With humble hope attend thy will,
And wait beneath thy feet.

H Y M N   CXIII.

Longing After Chriſt.

1 THOU ſhepherd of Iſrael, and mine,
    The joy, and deſire of my heart;
For cloſer communion I pine,
    I long to reſide where thou art:
The paſture I languiſh to find,
    Where all, who their ſhepherd obey,
Are fed, on thy boſom reclin'd,
    Are ſcreen'd from the heat of the day.

2 Ah! ſhew me that happieſt place,
    That place of thy people's abode;
Where ſaints in an extacy gaze,
    And hang on a crucify'd God:
Thy love for a ſinner declare,

Thy

Thy paffion and death on the tree;
My fpirit to Calvary bear,
To fuffer, and triumph with thee.

3 'Tis there with the lambs of thy flock,
   There only I covet to reft;
To lie at the foot of the rock,
   Or rife to be hid in thy breaft;
'Tis there I wou'd always abide,
   And never a moment depart,
Conceal'd in the cleft of thy fide,
   Eternally held in thine heart.

HYMN CXIV.

Chrift Withdrawn.

1 O What fhall I do to retrieve
     The love for a feafon beftow'd;
'Tis better to die than to live
   Exil'd from the prefence of God:
With forrow diftracted and doubt,
   With palpable horror oppreft,
The city I wander about,
   And feek my repofe in his breaft.

2 Ye watchmen of Ifrael, declare
   If ye my beloved have feen,
And point to that heav'nly fair,
   Surpaffing the children of men:
My lover and lord from above,

Who only can quiet my pain,
Whom only I languish to love,
O where shall I find him again?

3 The joy and desire of mine eyes,
 The end of my sorrow and woe;
My hope, and my heav'nly prize,
 My height of ambition below:
Once more if he shew me his face,
 He never again shall depart,
Detain'd in my closest embrace,
 Conceal'd in the depth of my heart.

HYMN CXV.

The Pilgrim's Song.

1 CHildren of the heav'nly king,
 As ye journey sweetly sing.
Sing your Saviour's worthy praise,
Glorious in his works and ways!

2 Ye are trav'ling home to God,
 In the way the fathers trod:
They are happy now, and ye
Soon their happiness shall see.

3 O ye banish'd seed be glad!
 Christ our advocate is made;
Us to save our flesh assumes,
Brother to our souls becomes.

4 Shout

4 Shout ye little flock and bleſt,
You on Jeſu's throne ſhall reſt,
There your ſeat is now prepar'd,
There your kingdom, and reward.

5 Fear not brethren joyful ſtand
On the borders of your land;
Jeſus Chriſt, your father's ſon,
Bids you joyfully come on.

6 Lord, obediently we'll go,
Gladly leaving all below;
Only thou our leader be,
And we ſtill will follow thee!

HYMN CXVI.

A bleſſed Goſpel.

1 BLEST are the ſouls that hear and know
  The goſpel's joyful ſound;
Peace ſhall attend the path they go,
  And light their ſteps ſurround.

2 Their joy ſhall bear their ſpirits up,
  Thro' their Redeemer's name;
His righteouſneſs exalts their hope,
  Nor Satan dares condemn.

3 The Lord our glory and defence,
  Strength, and ſalvation gives;

N   Iſrael

Israel, thy king for ever reigns,
  Thy God for ever lives.

HYMN CXVII.

1 GRACE! 'tis a charming sound,
    Harmonious to the ear!
  Heav'n with the echo shall resound,
    And all the earth shall hear.

2 Grace first contriv'd a way
    To save rebellious man;
  And all the steps, that grace display,
    Which drew the wondrous plan.

3 Grace taught my roving feet
    To tread the heav'nly road;
  And new supplies each hour I meet,
    While pressing on to God.

4 Grace all the work shall crown,
    Thro' everlasting days,
  It lays in heav'n the topmost stone;
    And well deserves the praise.

HYMN CXVIII.

1 COME, descend, O heav'nly Spirit,
    Fan each spark into a flame,
  Blessings let us now inherit,
    Blessings that we cannot name

Whilst

Whilst hosannas we are singing,
  May our hearts in rapture move,
Feel new grace in them still springing,
  Breathe the air of purest love.

2 Let us sail in grace's ocean
  Float on that unbounded sea,
Guided into pure devotion,
  Kept from paths of error free:
On thy heav'nly manna feeding,
  Screen'd from every envious foe;
Love, O love for sinners bleeding
  All for thee we would forego.

3 Keep us, Lord still in communion,
  Daily nearer drawn to thee;
Sinking in the sweetest union
  Of that heart-felt mystery:
Keep us safe from each delusion,
  Well protected from all harms;
Free from sin and all confusion,
  Circle us within thy arms.

HYMN CXIX.

Rejoice evermore.

1 REJOICE evermore
    With Angels above,
In Jesus's pow'r,
  In Jesus's love;
With glad exultation
  Your triumph proclaim,

Ascribing

Ascribing salvation
To God, and the Lamb.

2 Thou, Lord, our relief
In trouble haſt been,
Haſt ſav'd us from grief,
Haſt ſav'd us from ſin,
The pow'r of thy ſpirit
Can ſet our hearts free;
And we ſhall inherit
All fulneſs in thee.

3 All fulneſs of peace,
All fulneſs of joy,
And ſpiritual bliſs
That never can cloy,
To us it is given
In Jeſus to know,
A kingdom of heaven,
A heaven below.

4 No longer we join
Where ſinners invite,
Nor envy the ſwine
Their brutiſh delight;
Their joy is all ſadneſs,
Their mirth is all vain,
Their laughter is madneſs,
Their pleaſure is pain.

5 O may they at last
  With sorrow return,
The pleasure to taste,
  For which they were born!
Our Jesus receiving,
  Our happiness prove,
The joy of believing,
  The heaven of love.

HYMN CXX.

Redeeming love.

1 COME heav'nly love, inspire my song,
    With thy immortal flame;
  And teach my heart, and teach my tongue,
    The Saviour's lovely name.

2 The Saviour! O what endless charms
    Dwell in the blissful sound!
  Its influence ev'ry fear disarms,
    And spreads sweet comfort round.

3 Here pardon, life, and joys divine
    In rich effusion flow,
  For guilty rebels lost in sin,
    And doom'd to endless woe.

4 God's only Son, (stupendous grace!)
    Forsook his throne above;
  And swift to save our wretched race,
    He flew on wings of love.

5 Th'

5 Th' almighty former of the skies
    Stoop'd to our vile abode;
While angels view'd with wond'ring eyes,
    And hail'd th' incarnate God.

6 O the rich depths of love divine!
    Of bliss, a boundless store:
Dear Saviour, let me call thee mine.
    I cannot wish for more.

7 On thee alone my hope relies,
    Beneath thy cross I fall,
My Lord, my life, my sacrifice,
    My Saviour, and my all.

H Y M N CXXI.

Christian Love

1   LET party names no more
        The christian world o'erspread;
Gentile and Jew, and bond and free
    Are one in Christ their head.

2   Among the saints on earth,
        Let mutual love be found;
Heirs of the same inheritance,
    With mutual blessings crown'd.

3   Let envy and ill-will
        Be banish'd far away;
Those should in strictest friendship dwell,

Who

Who the fame Lord obey.

4 Thus will the church below
Refemble that above,
Where ftreams of pleafure ever flow,
And ev'ry heart is love.

HYMN CXXII.

The Myfteries of Providence.

1 LORD, how myfterious are thy ways!
How blind are we, how mean our praife!
Thy fteps can mortal eyes explore?
'Tis ours to wonder, and adore.

2 Thy deep decrees from creature fight,
Are hid in fhades of awful night;
Amid the lines, with curious eye,
Not angel minds prefume to pry.

3 Great God, I would not afk to fee,
What in futurity fhall be;
If light and blifs attend my days,
Then let my future hours be praife.

4 Is darknefs and diftrefs my fhare?
Then let me truft thy guardian care;
Enough for me, if love divine
At length thro' ev'ry cloud fhall fhine.

5 Yet this my foul defires to know,
Be this my only wifh below;
" That

"That Chrift is mine!"---this great requeft
Grant, bounteous God---and I am bleft.

HYMN CXXIII.

Winter.

1 SEE how rude winter's icy hand
   Has ftript the trees, and feal'd the ground;
   But fpring fhall foon his rage withftand,
   And fpread new beauties all around.

2 My foul a fharper winter mourns,
   Barren and lifelefs I remain,
   When will the gentle fpring return,
   And bid my graces grow again?

3 Jefus, my glorious fun, arife,
   'Tis thine the frozen heart to move;
   Oh! hufh thefe ftorms, and clear my fkies,
   And let me feel thy vital love.

4 Dear Lord, regard my feeble cry,
   I faint and droop 'till thou appear;
   Wilt thou permit thy plant to die?
   Muft it be winter all the year?

5 Be ftill, my foul, and wait his hour,
   With humble pray'r, and patient faith,
   'Till he reveals his gracious pow'r,
   Repofe on what his promife faith.

6 He, by whofe all commanding words,
                           Seafons

Seasons their changing course maintain;
In ev'ry change a pledge affords,
That none shall seek his face in vain.

HYMN CXXIV.

True happiness.

1 HOW happy is the christian's state!
    His sins are all forgiven;
A cheering ray confirms the grace,
    And lifts his hopes to heav'n.

2 Tho' in the rugged path of life,
    He heaves the pensive sigh;
Yet trusting in his God he finds
    Deliv'ring grace is nigh.

3 If, to prevent his wand'ring steps,
    He feels the chast'ning rod;
The gentle stroke shall bring him back
    To his forgiving God.

4 And when the welcome message comes
    To call his soul away;
His soul, in raptures shall ascend
    To everlasting day.

HYMN CXXV.

1 O Let thy love our hearts constrain,
    Jesus, the crucify'd!

What haſt thou done our hearts to gain?
  Languiſh'd, and groan'd, and dy'd!

2 Us into cloſeſt union draw,
    And in our inward parts
  Let kindneſs ſweetly write her law,
    Let love command our hearts.

3 Who would not now purſue the way,
    Where Jeſu's footſteps ſhine?
  Who would not own the pleaſing ſway
    Of charity divine?

4 O let us find the ancient way,
    Our wond'ring foes to move,
  And force a frowning world to ſay,
    " See how theſe chriſtians love!"

HYMN CXXVI.

Evening.

1 GLORY to thee, my God, this night,
    For all the bleſſings of the light;
  Keep me, O keep me, King of kings,
  Under thine own almighty wings.

2 Forgive me, Lord, for thy dear ſon,
  Whatever ills this day I've done;
  That with the world, myſelf, and thee,
  I, 'ere I ſleep, at peace may be.

3 Teach

3 Teach me to live, that I may dread
 The grave as little as my bed;
 Teach me to die, that so I may
 Triumphing rise at the last day.

4 O may my soul on thee repose,
 And with sweet sleep my eye-lids close;
 Sleep that may me more vig'rous make,
 To serve my God when I awake.

5 Let my blest guardian, while I sleep,
 Close to my bed his vigils keep;
 Let no vain dreams disturb my rest,
 Nor pow'rs of darkness me molest.

6 Praise God from whom all blessings flow,
 Praise him all creatures here below;
 Praise him above, ye heav'nly host,
 Praise Father, Son, and Holy Ghost.

HYMN CXXVII.

Lord's day morning.

1 TO-DAY God bids the faithful rest,
   To-day he show'rs his grace;
 "Seek ye my face," the Lord hath said,
 Lord, we will seek thy face.

2 Come, let us leave the things of earth,
 With God's assembly join;

Lo!

Lo! heav'n defcends to welcome man,
 To tafte the things divine!

3 We come, dear Saviour, lo! we come,
    Lord of our life and foul;
  We come difeas'd, and faint, and fick,
    Be pleas'd to make us whole.

4 We thirft, and fly to thee, O Lord,
    Thou fountain-head of good;
  Filthy we come, and all unclean,
    O cleanfe us in thy blood.

5 O may we pleafe our God to day,
    May that be all our care!
  Give, Lord, thy grace, left evil thoughts
    Should mingle in our pray'r.

6 Amid th' affembly of thy faints,
    Let us be faithful found;
  And let us join in humble pray'r,
    And in thy praife abound.

7 Let thy good fpirit help our fouls,
    With faith thy word to hear;.
  Be with us in thy temple, Lord,
    And let us find thee near.

H Y M N   CXXVIII.

Lord's day Evening.

1 WHEN, O dear Jefus, when fhall I
      Behold thee all ferene?
  Bleft in perpetual fabbath-day,
    Without a veil between?

2 Affift me while I wander here,
    Amidft a world of cares;   Incline

Incline my heart to pray with love,
And then accept my pray'rs

3 Releafe my foul from ev'ry chain,
No more hell's captive led;
And pardon a repenting child,
For whom the Saviour bled.

4 Spare me, O God, O fpare the foul,
That gives it felf to thee;
Take all that I poffefs below,
And give thyfelf to me.

5 Thy fpirit, O my father, give,
To be my guide and friend,
To light my way to ceafelefs joys,
Where fabbaths never end.

HYMN CXXIX.

Morning.

1 AWAKE, my foul, and with the fun,
Thy daily ftage of duty run;
Shake off dull floth, and early rife
To pay thy morning facrifice.

2 Redeem thy mis-fpent time that's paft,
Live this day as if 'twere thy laft;
T' improve thy talents take due care,
'Gainft the great-day thyfelf prepare.

O   3 Let

3 Let all thy converse be sincere,
   Thy conscience as the noon-day clear;
   Think how th' all-seeing God thy ways,
   And ev'ry secret thought surveys.

4 Glory to God, who safe hath kept,
   And hath refresh'd me while I slept;
   Grant, Lord, when I from death shall wake,
   I may of endless life partake.

5 Direct, controul, suggest this day,
   All I design, or do, or say;
   That all my pow'rs, with all their might,
   In thy sole glory may unite.

6 Praise God, from whom all blessings flow,
   Praise him all creatures here below;
   Praise him above, ye heav'nly host,
   Praise Father, Son, and Holy Ghost.

HYMN CXXX.

1 BEFORE Jehovah's awful throne,
   Ye nations bow with sacred joy;
   Know that the Lord is God alone,
   He can create, and he destroy.

2 His sov'reign pow'r, without our aid,
   Made us of clay, and form'd us men.
   And when like wand'ring sheep we stray'd,
   He brought us to his fold again.

3 We'll

3 We'll crow'd thy gates with thankful fongs,
   High as the heav'ns our voices raife;
   And earth with her ten thoufand tongues
   Shall fill thy courts with founding praife.

4 Wide as the world is thy command,
   Vaft as eternity thy love;
   Firm as a rock thy truth muft ftand,
   When rolling years fhall ceafe to move.

HYMN CXXXI.

For New Year's Day.

1 AND now my foul, another year
      Of thy fhort life is paft;
   I cannot long continue here,
      And this may be my laft.

2 Much of my dubious life is gone,
      Nor will return again;
   And fwift my paffing moments run,
      The few that yet remain.

3 Awake, my foul, with utmoft care
      Thy true condition learn;
   What are thy hopes, how fure, how fair,
      And what thy great concern!

4 Now a new fcene of time begins,
      Set out afrefh for heav'n;

Seek

Seek pardon for thy former sins,
　In Christ so freely giv'n.

5　Devoutly yield thyself to God,
　　And on his grace depend;
　With zeal pursue the heav'nly road,
　　Nor doubt a happy end.

HYMN CXXXII.

Another.

1　THE Lord of earth and sky,
　　　The God of ages praise!
　Who reigns enthron'd on high,
　　　Ancient of endless days,
　Who lengthens out our trial here,
　And spares us yet another year.

2　　Barren and wither'd trees,
　　　　We cumber'd long the ground;
　　No fruit of holiness
　　　　On our dead souls was found;
　Yet did he us in mercy spare,
　Another, and another year.

3　　When justice bar'd the sword,
　　　　To cut the fig tree down,
　　The pity of our Lord
　　　　Cry'd---" Let it still alone:"

The

The father mild inclin'd his ear,
And spar'd us yet another year.

4 Jesus, thy speaking blood
     From God obtain'd the grace,
   Who therefore hath bestow'd
     On us a longer space:
   Thou didst in our behalf appear,
   And lo! we see another year.

5 Then dig about our root,
     Break up our fallow ground,
   And let our gracious fruit
     To thy great praise abound;
   O let us all thy praise declare,
   And fruit unto perfection bear.

HYMN CXXXIII.

It is finished.

1 "'TIS finish'd," the Redeemer said,
   And meekly bow'd his dying head,
     Whilst we this sentence scan,
   Come, sinners, and observe the word,
   Behold the conquests of the Lord,
     Compleat for helpless man.

2 Finish'd the righteousness of grace,
   Finish'd for sinners pard'ning peace;
     Their mighty debt is paid:

Accusing

Accusing law cancell'd by blood,
And wrath of an offended God
　In sweet oblivion laid.

3 Who now shall urge a second claim?
The law no longer can condemn,
　Faith a release can shew:
Justice itself a friend appears,
The prison-house a whisper hears,
　"Loose him, and let him go."

4 O unbelief, injurious bar!
Source of tormenting, fruitless fear,
　Why dost thou yet reply?
Where'er thy loud objections fall,
"'Tis finish'd," still may answer all,
　And silence ev'ry cry.

5 His toil divinely finish'd stands,
But ah! the praise his work demands,
　Careful may we attend!
Conclusion to our souls be this,
Because salvation finish'd is,
　Our thanks shall never end.

HYMN CXXXIV.

1 CHRIST the Lord is ris'n to-day,
　Sons of men and angels say!
Raise your joys and triumphs high,
Sing, ye heav'ns, and earth reply.

2 Love's

2 Love's redeeming work is done,
  Fought the fight, the battle won;
  Lo! our sun's eclipse is o'er,
  Lo! he sets in blood no more.

3 Vain the stone, the watch, the seal,
  Christ hath burst the gates of hell:
  Death in vain forbids his rise,
  Christ hath open'd paradise.

4 Lives again our glorious King,
  Where, O death, is now thy sting?
  Once he dy'd our souls to save,
  Where's thy victory, O grave?

5 Soar we now where Christ hath led,
  Foll'wing our exalted Head;
  Made like him, like him we rise,
  Ours the cross, the grave, the skies.

6 What tho' once we perish'd all,
  Partners of our parents fall;
  Second life we all receive,
  In our heav'nly Adam live.

7 Hail the Lord of earth and heav'n!
  Praise to thee by both be giv'n!
  Thee we greet triumphant now,
  Hail the resurrection—thou!

8 King of glory! soul of bliss!
  Everlasting life is this—

Thee to know---thy pow'r to prove,
Thus to sing, and thus to love.

HYMN CXXXV.

God glorious, and Sinners saved.

1 FATHER, how wide thy glory shines!
    How high thy wonders rise!
Known thro' the earth by thousand signs,
    By thousands thro' the skies.

2 Those mighty Orbs proclaim thy pow'r,
    Their motions speak thy skill;
And on the wings of ev'ry hour
    We read thy patience still.

3 Part of thy name divinely stands
    On all thy creatures writ,
They shew the labour of thy hands,
    The impress of thy feet.

4 But when we view thy grand design
    To save rebellious worms,
Where wisdom pow'r and goodness shine,
    In their most glorious forms;

5 Our thoughts are lost in rev'rend awe;
    We love, and we adore;
The holy Angels never saw
    So much of GOD before.

6 Here God hath made his nature known,
    And thought can never trace,
Which of his glories brightest shone,
    In our Redeemer's face.

7 O the sweet myst'ries of that Cross
    Where Jesus lov'd and dy'd!
Her noblest life my spirit draws
    From his dear wounded side.

8 Now the full glories of the LAMB
    Adorn the heav'nly plains;
Sweet Cherubs learn Immanuel's name,
    And try their choicest strains.

9 O may I bear some humble part
    In that immortal song!
Wonder and joy shall tune my heart,
    And love command my tongue.

HYMN CXXXVI.

Love on a Cross, and a Throne.

1 NOW let my faith grow strong, and rise,
    And view my LORD in all his love;
Look back to hear his dying cries,
Then mount and see his throne above.

2 See where he languish'd on the Cross;
Beneath my sins he groan'd and dy'd;
See where he sits to plead my cause,
By his Almighty Father's side.

3 If I behold his bleeding heart,
  There love in floods of sorrow reigns,
  He triumphs o'er the killing smart,
  And buys my pleasure with his pains.

4 Or if I climb th' eternal hills,
  Where the dear CONQU'ROR sits enthron'd,
  Still in his heart compassion dwells,
  Near the memorials of his wound.

5 How shall a pardon'd rebel show
  How much I love my SAVIOUR GOD?
  LORD here I banish ev'ry foe,
  I hate the sins that cost thy blood.

6 I hold no more commerce with hell,
  My dearest lusts shall all depart;
  But let thine image ever dwell
  Stampt as a seal upon my heart.

HYMN CXXXVII.

Desiring to love CHRIST.

1 COME let me love; or is my mind
  Harden'd to stone, or froze to ice!
  I see the blessed fair one bend,
  And stoop t' embrace me from the skies.

2 O! 'tis a thought would melt a rock,
  And make an heart of iron move,

That those sweet lips, that heav'nly look,
Should seek and wish a mortal's love.

3 I was a traytor doom'd to fire,
Bound to sustain eternal pains;
He flew on wings of strong desire,
Assum'd my guilt, and took my chains.

4 Infinite grace! Almighty Charms!
Stand in amaze, O earth and skies!
JESUS the GOD with naked arms,
Hangs on a Cross of love and dies.

5 Did pity ever stoop so low,
Dress'd in divinity and blood?
Was ever rebel courted so
With groans of an expiring GOD?

6 Again he lives, and spreads his hands,
Hands that were nail'd to tort'ring smart;
By these dear wounds, says he; and stands
And prays to clasp me to his heart.

7 Sure I must love; or are my ears
Still deaf, nor will my passions move;
Then let me melt this heart to tears;
This heart shall yield to death or love.

HYMN CXXXVIII.

1 THE Sun of righteousness appears,
To set in blood no more!

Adore

Adore the scatt'rer of your fears,
　　Your rising sun adore.

2　The saints, when he resign'd his breath,
　　Unclos'd their sleeping eyes;
　He breaks again the bands of death,
　　Again the dead arise.

3　Alone the dreadful race he ran,
　　Alone the wine-press trod;
　He dy'd, and suffer'd as a man,
　　He rises as a God.

4　In vain the stone, the watch, the seal,
　　Forbid an early rise,
　To him who breaks the gates of hell,
　　And opens paradise.

HYMN CXXXIX.

1　O For a sweet inspiring ray,
　　To animate our feeble strains,
　From the bright realms of endless day,
　The blissful realms, where Jesus reigns!

2　There low before his glorious throne,
　　Adoring saints and angels fall,
　And with delightful worship own
　　His smile their bliss, their heav'n, their all.

3　Immortal glories crown his head,
　　While tuneful hallelujahs rise;

And

And love, and joy, and triumph spread
Thro' all th' assemblies of the skies.

4 He smiles, and seraphs tune their songs,
To boundless rapture while they gaze;
Ten thousand thousand joyful tongues
Resound his everlasting praise.

5 There all the ransom'd of the Lamb
Shall join at last the heav'nly choir;
O may the joy-inspiring theme
Awake our faith, and warm desire!

6 Dear Saviour, let thy spirit seal
Our int'rest in that blissful place;
'Till death remove this mortal veil,
And we behold thy lovely face.

HYMN CXL.

1 COME, thou long expected Jesus!
 Born to set thy people free;
From our fears and sins release us,
 Let us find our rest in thee!
Israel's strength and consolation,
 Hope of all the earth thou art;
Dear desire of ev'ry nation,
 Joy of ev'ry longing heart!

2 Born thy people to deliver,
 Born a child, and yet a king;

Born to reign in us for ever,
  Now thy gracious kingdom bring!
By thine own eternal Spirit,
  Rule in all our hearts alone;
By thine all-sufficient merit,
  Raise us to thy glorious throne.

HYMN CXLI.

On the Death of a Believer.

1 'TIS finish'd, 'tis done!
    The spirit is fled,
  The pris'ner is gone,
    The christian is dead:
  The christian is living
    Thro' Jesus his love,
  And gladly receiving
    A kingdom above.

2 All honour and praise
    Is Jesus's due;
  Supported by grace,
    He fought his way thro':
  Triumphantly glorious,
    Thro' Jesus's zeal,
  And more than victorious
    O'er sin, death, and hell.

3 Then let us record
    The conquering name,

Our

Our Captain and Lord
  With shoutings proclaim :
Who trust in his passion,
  And follow our Head,
To certain salvation,
  They all shall be led.

4 O Jesus, lead on
  Thy militant care,
And give us the crown
  Of righteousness there :
Where dazzled with glory,
  The seraphim gaze,
Or prostrate adore thee
  In silence of praise.

5 Come, Lord, and display
  Thy sign in the sky,
And bear us away
  To mansions on high :
The kingdom be given,
  The purchase divine,
And crown us in heaven
  Eternally thine.

HYMN CXLII.

Sins and sorrows laid before GOD.

1 O that I knew the secret place
    Where I might find my God!

I'd spread my wants before his face,
And pour my woes abroad.

I'd tell him how my sins arise,
What sorrows I sustain,
How grace decays, and comfort dies,
And leaves my heart in pain:

3 I'd say how flesh and sense rebel,
What inward foes combine,
With this vain world and pow'rs of hell,
To vex this heart of mine.

4 He knows what arguments I'd take
To wrestle with my God;
I'd plead for his own mercy's sake,
And for my Saviour's blood.

5 My God will pity my complaints,
And heal my broken bones;
He takes the meaning of his saints,
The language of their groans.

6 Arise my Soul from deep distress,
And banish ev'ry fear;
He calls thee to his throne of grace,
To spread thy sorrows there.

H Y M N

HYMN CXLIII.

The presence of GOD *worth dying for.*

1 LORD, 'tis an infinite delight
   To see thy lovely face,
To dwell whole ages in thy sight,
   And feel thy vital rays.

2 This Gabriel knows; and sings thy name
   With raptures on his tongue;
Moses the saint enjoys the same,
   And heav'n repeats the song.

3 While the bright nation sounds thy praise
   From each eternal hill,
Sweet odours of exhaling grace
   The happy region fill.

4 Thy love, a sea without a shore,
   Spreads life and joy abroad;
O 'tis a heav'n worth dying for
   To see a smiling GOD.

5 Shew me thy face, and I'll away
   From all inferior things;
Speak, LORD, and here I quit my clay,
   And stretch my airy wings.

6 Sweet was the journey to the Sky
   The wondrous prophet try'd;
" Climb up the mount, (says GOD) and die;"
   The Prophet climb'd and dy'd.

7 Softly

7 Softly his fainting head he lay
 Upon his Maker's breast;
 His Maker kiss'd his soul away,
 And laid his flesh to rest.

8 In God's own arms he left the breath
 That God's own spirit gave;
 His was the noblest road to death,
 And his the sweetest grave.

HYMN CXLIV.

A sight of heaven in sickness.

1 OFT have I sat in secret sighs,
 To feel my flesh decay,
 Then groan'd aloud with frighted eyes,
 To view the tott'ring clay.

2 But I forbid my sorrows now,
 Nor dares the flesh complain;
 Diseases bring their profit too;
 The joy o'ercomes the pain.

3 My chearful soul now all the day
 Sits waiting here and sings;
 Looks thro' the ruins of her clay,
 And practises her wings.

4 Faith almost changes into sight,
 While from afar she spies,
 Her fair inheritance, in light
 Above created Skies.

5 Had

5 Had but the prison walls been strong,
    And firm without a flaw,
  In darkness she had dwelt too long,
    And less of glory saw:

6 But now the everlasting hills
    Thro' ev'ry chink appear,
  And something of the joy she feels
    While she's a prisoner here:

7 The shines of heav'n rush sweetly in
    At all the gaping flaws;
  Visions of endless bliss are seen
    And native air she draws.

8 O may these walls stand tott'ring still,
    The breaches never close!
  If I must here in darkness dwell,
    And all this glory lose!

9 Or rather let this flesh decay,
    The ruins wider grow,
  Till glad to see th' enlarged way,
    I stretch my pinions through.

HYMN CXLV.

Ascending to Christ in heaven.

1 'TIS pure delight, without alloy,
    Jesus, to hear thy name,
  My spirit leaps with inward joy,
    I feel the sacred flame.

2 My

2 My paſſions hold a pleaſing reign
   While love inſpires my breaſt,
Love the divineſt of the train,
   The ſov'reign of the reſt.

3 This is the grace muſt live and ſing,
   When faith and fear ſhall ceaſe,
Muſt found from ev'ry joyful ſtring,
   Thro' the ſweet groves of bliſs.

4 Let life immortal ſeize my clay;
   Let love refine my blood;
Her flames can bear my ſoul away,
   Can bring me near my GOD.

5 Sink down ye ſeparating hills,
   Let guilt and death remove,
'Tis love that drives my Chariot wheels,
   And death muſt yield to love.

HYMN CXLVI.

A proſpect of the Reſurrection.

1 HOW long ſhall death the tyrant reign,
   And triumph o'er the juſt,
While the rich blood of martyrs ſlain
   Lies mingled with the duſt?

2 When ſhall the tedious night be gone?
   When will our Lord appear?
Our fond deſires would pray him down,
   Our love embrace him here.

3 Let faith arife, and climb the hills,
    And from afar defcry
How diftant are his Chariot wheels,
    And tell how faft they fly.

4 Lo, I behold the fcatt'ring fhades,
    The dawn of heav'n appears,
The fweet immortal morning fpreads
    Its blufhes round the fpheres.

5 I fee the Lord of glory come,
    And flaming guards around!
The Skies divide to make him room,
    The trumpet fhakes the ground.

6 I hear the voice! " Ye dead arife;"
    And lo, the graves obey,
And waking Saints with joyful eyes
    Salute th' expected day.

7 They leave the duft, and on the wing
    Rife to the middle air,
In fhining garments meet their king,
    And low adore him there.

8 O may my humble fpirit ftand
    Amongft them cloth'd in white!
The meaneft place at his right hand
    Is infinite delight.

9 How will our joy and wonder rife,
    When our returning king
Shall bear us homeward thro' the fkies
    On love's triumphant wing!

HYMN

HYMN CXLVII.

An HYMN for the American States.

1 GIVE thanks to God, your King,
And speak his worthy fame:
Your highest honours bring
To his almighty name:
For God hath made his MERCIES known;
And call'd AMERICA his own.

2 Record the wonders wrought
By his victorious hand,
Which hath deliv'rance brought
To our distressed land;
For God hath made his WONDERS known;
And call'd this WESTERN LAND his own.

3 He brought our Fathers o'er
The vast Atlantic Sea,
To this delightful shore,
The land of Liberty:
For God hath made his GOODNESS known;
And call'd COLUMBIA his own.

4 He drove the heathen out,
Before his people's face;
Put savage bands to rout,
And gave to us their place:
For God hath made his *Judgements* known;
And call'd this NEW-FOUND-LAND his own.

5 He

5 He made us to pofsefs
  A country long conceal'd;
  And turn'd the wildernefs
  Into a fruitful field:
  For God hath made his KINDNESS known;
  And call'd this INFANT-LAND his own.

6 He made us to increafe
  In numbers, wealth, and ftrength;
  And gave a fettled peace
  Unto the land at length;
  For God hath made his POWER known;
  And call'd this FRUITFUL-LAND his own.

7 His gofpel forth he fent
  To teach the way to heav'n;
  His pow'r attending went,
  To fhew our fins forgiv'n:
  For God hath made SALVATION known;
  And call'd the SOULS OF MEN his own.

8 Long time our land enjoy'd
  Peace, plenty, health, and gain;
  And when we were annoy'd,
  The Lord did us fuftain;
  For God hath made DELIV'RANCE known;
  And call'd the FEEBLE FOLK his own.

9 When pow'rful foes oppreft
  Us round on ev'ry fide,
  The Lord this people bleft
  With fkilful men to guide;

For

_For God hath made his WISDOM known;
And call'd thefe RISING STATES his own.

10 Our foes our ruin fought,
  Which they could not obtain;
  By providence they're taught
  That pride of Man is vain:
  For God hath made his JUSTICE known;
  And call'd the RIGHTEOUS CAUSE his own.

11 God made the feeble ftand
  Againft their boafted pow'r;
  And gave them not our land,
  To fpoil and to devour.
  For God hath made PROTECTION known;
  And call'd FAIR FREEDOM'S LAND his own.

12 JEHOVAH peace ordains,
  The noife of battle's o'er,
  No blood the vefture ftains,
  Nor thund'ring cannon roar;
  For God hath made his GLORY known;
  And call'd the FAVOUR'D STATES his own.

13 Now let our land enjoy
  Peace, plenty, liberty;
  Let war no more annoy,
  Amen, fo let it be.
  Lord, make thy LOVING FAVOUR known;
  And call this CONTINENT thine own.

F I N I S.

www.ingramcontent.com/pod-product-compliance
Lightning Source LLC
Chambersburg PA
CBHW020250170426
43202CB00008B/304